Route 66
ROADSIDE
SIGNS
@ND
ADVERTISEMENTS

Joe Sonderman

PHOTOGRAPHY BY

Joe Sonderman
and Jim Hinckley

VOYAGEUR
PRESS

Blue Swallow
MOTEL
100%
REFRIGERATED
AIR
VACANCY
TV
LOBBY
OPEN
HISTORIC
PROPERTY
+
INSPECTION
INVITED
+
TRUCK & RV
PARKING

Quarto is the authority on a wide range of topics.

Quarto educates, entertains and enriches the lives of our readers—enthusiasts and lovers of hands-on living.

www.quartoknows.com

First published in 2016 by Voyageur Press, an imprint of Quarto Publishing Group USA Inc., 400 First Avenue North, Suite 400, Minneapolis, MN 55401 USA.
Telephone: (612) 344-8100 Fax: (612) 344-8692

quartoknows.com
Visit our blogs at quartoknows.com

Voyageur Press titles are also available at discounts in bulk quantity for industrial or sales-promotional use. For details contact the Special Sales Manager at Quarto Publishing Group USA Inc., 400 First Avenue North, Suite 400, Minneapolis, MN 55401 USA.

10 9 8 7 6 5 4 3 2 1

ISBN: 978-0-7603-4974-8

Library of Congress Cataloging-in-Publication Data

Names: Sonderman, Joe, author. | Hinckley, Jim, 1958- photographer.
Title: Route 66 roadside signs and advertisements / Joe Sonderman ; photographs by Jim Hinckley.
Description: Minneapolis, MN : Voyageur Press, 2016.
Identifiers: LCCN 2016020073 | ISBN 9780760349748 (paperback)
Subjects: LCSH: United States Highway 66--History--Pictorial works. | Roadside architecture--United States--History--Pictorial works. | BISAC: DESIGN / Graphic Arts / Advertising. | TRAVEL / United States / West / Mountain (AZ, CO, ID, MT, NM, UT, WY). | ANTIQUES & COLLECTIBLES / Americana.
Classification: LCC HE356.U55 S667 2016 | DDC 659.13/42--dc23
LC record available at https://lccn.loc.gov/2016020073

Acquiring Editor: Todd R. Berger
Project Manager: Caitlin Fultz
Art Director: Cindy Samargia Laun
Cover Design: Kent Jensen
Book Design and Layout: Rebecca Pagel

Printed in China

On the front cover: Elementallmaging/Getty Images
On the frontispiece: Vintage neon Route 66 sign. *Kris Schmidt/Shutterstock*
On the title pages: The Blue Swallow Motel in Tucumcari, New Mexico, lights up the night sky. *Brian S./Shutterstock*
On the contents pages: Metal Route 66 sign under the Arizona sun. *Mike Flippo/Shutterstock*

Dedication

In memory of Bob Waldmire, Tom Teague, Lucille Hammons, Lillian Redman, Jack Rittenhouse, Hugh and Zelta Davis, Bill Shea, "Sunday John" Dausch, and those who came before. With thanks to Michael Wallis, Jim Ross, Shellee Graham, Jerry McClanahan, Cheryl Jett, Roamin Rich, Nick Gerlich, David Wickline, and all of the authors and photographers who make us want to come back today.

Acknowledgments

Special thanks to Jim and Judy Hinckley, who, along with Jeroen and Maggie Boersma, shared dozens of their amazing photos for this project. Also thanks to Mike Ward and Steve Rider, who have helped me on so many projects, and to Nancy and Tom Mueller at the Blue Swallow in Tucumcari, New Mexico. Thanks Lorraine, Cathy, and Kim Sonderman, and to the staff at the MoDOT TMC in Chesterfield, Missouri.

Contents

Introduction

The glory years of Route 66 and of the neon sign coincided. They faded at the same time and are both being revived today. On Route 66, it was possible to drive for hours seeing only the occasional headlights. So when the car topped a hill above a town, the neon lights seemed to set the sky ablaze. They flashed and twirled in bright color and the romantic images evoked the history and scenery of the region. It was all a show, designed to catch the traveler's eye at high speed. America was on the move, and neon captured the excitement of "going somewhere."

But even during the glory years, change was in the air. The interstates took traffic away from the main streets, and the big chains with their standardized corporate signage sprouted along the off-ramps. It was all neat and tidy, sanitized for our protection. The interstate made Route 66 obsolete, and neon was seen as trashy and tacky. The signs came down or remained next to an abandoned property at the mercy of vandals and the weather. But interest in Route 66 is at an all-time high, and neon is now seen as an art form.

There is still a certain type of person who searches for Route 66 and is drawn to the glow of the neon like a moth to a flame. For some, it is a yearning for a simpler time or memories of childhood vacations. Others actively seek out something that the rest of society sees as old and kitschy. And there are those of us who find time is precious, that the journey is as important as the destination. Paraphrasing Charles Kuralt, the interstate highway system made it possible to drive across the country and not see anything. That's fine when folks are in a hurry. But it is costing us our sense of community. The same chain restaurants, hotels, and big-box retailers cluster at every interstate off-ramp. There is no sense of place. Sometimes, life is best savored at a slower pace and begins at the off-ramp.

Roy's Motel and Café along Route 66 in Amboy, California. *Gimas/Shutterstock*

The Wagon Wheel Motel in Cuba is among the best-preserved classic Route 66 motels. It opened in 1934 as the Wagon Wheel Cabins, operated by Robert and Margaret Martin. John and Winifred Pratt ran the motel from 1947 to 1963, when Pauline Roberts and her husband took over. Connie Eichols has since restored the motel to its former glory—with modern amenities.

Other signs along Route 66 weren't as glamorous or as flashy as those with neon. These were the signs that kept us on the right track, warned of danger, or built anticipation for the attractions down the road, sometimes hundreds of miles away. Those were the banners with the comely cowgirl, the giant jackrabbit, or Jesse James with his steely eyes peering from behind a mask. The kids would be begging to see the Jesse James hideout at Meramec Caverns after seeing the billboards and the slogan painted on barn roofs for hundreds of miles.

One of the most famous signs in the world is the simple Route 66 shield. But it was a long road to get to that point. As the automobile age began, road building was usually a local affair. Once Henry Ford put an entire nation on wheels, the new travelers demanded better roads and better signage. Private promoters stepped in to lay out highways of their own. They gave the routes glamorous names such as the Lincoln Highway, Dixie Highway, or National Old Trails Route, but often spent little on maintenance. Merchants and towns made "contributions" to have a highway pass their front door, leading hapless motorists miles out of their way.

Fence posts, phone poles, barns, and nearly every available space beside the road would be painted in a confusing array of colors and symbols used to identify these "highways." The routes often overlapped. In 1925 the federal government moved to eliminate the confusing patchwork of private and state routes. A committee appointed by the Department of Agriculture assigned even numbers to the proposed east-west federal highways with the most important ending in "0." The route between Chicago and Los Angeles was designated as "60," due mainly to the efforts of Cyrus Avery. But Governor William Fields of Kentucky demanded that "60" be assigned to the route through his state. After a battle of angry telegrams, Avery and his supporters agreed to accept the catchy-sounding "66" on April 30, 1926. The numbering system became official on November 11, 1926.

Route 66 became the most famous route in the world in part because it had its own publicity machine. The US 66 Highway Association immediately went to work to put it on the map. Press releases flowed and the entire nation followed an epic transcontinental footrace dubbed the "Bunion Derby" that followed the entire length of 66 in 1928.

The route became even more ingrained in our culture with the release of John Steinbeck's novel *The Grapes of Wrath*. The highway will forever be associated with images of the desperate people snubbed as "Okies" with everything they own strapped to an overheated jalopy. The glory years of 66 came after World War II, when Nat King Cole's "(Get Your Kicks on) Route 66" hit the charts. The beat poets and the television show *Route 66*, which seldom filmed anywhere near the route, added to the romance. Route 66 became a symbol of freedom and adventure.

The science behind the neon sign can be traced back to before the age of electricity. But it was French inventor Georges Claude who developed the electrode that made the use of neon gas in a vacuum tube possible. He unveiled his invention at the Paris Exposition of 1910, and Paris was quickly ablaze in what the public called "neon fire." The first neon signs in America stopped traffic when they were installed atop a Los Angeles Packard dealership in 1923.

It was in Las Vegas that neon reached its peak, at the same time Route 66 was enjoying its halcyon years as well. Downtown Las Vegas was dubbed "Glitter Gulch." Tom Wolfe wrote, "One can look at Las Vegas from a mile away on Route 91 and see no buildings, no trees, only signs. But such signs! They tower, they revolve, they oscillate, and they soar in shapes before which the existing vocabulary of art history is helpless." The same scene was repeated on a smaller scale in Chicago, St. Louis, Tulsa, Oklahoma City, Albuquerque, and Los Angeles, and on every main street in between.

Today, businesses are trying to recapture that look, and collectors eagerly, many times too eagerly, seek them out. Vintage porcelain neon signs are seldom found anymore in their original settings. Those that remain are being restored, and new signs with a vintage look go up every day. Of course, now there is LED lighting that is cheap and easier to protect from weather and vandals. But for some, only the buzzing, deep-hued neon signs will do. Route 66 associations from Illinois to California are working to preserve and restore these once-brilliant roadside relics.

So let's hit the road! We will see signs that are gone but not forgotten, witness the faded glory of those awaiting restoration, and follow the familiar 66 shield. These are the signs of Route 66.

Chapter 1

The Beginnings

Standing on the shore of Lake Michigan, with the breeze behind one's back, more than two thousand miles (3,220 kilometers) of adventure and history are ahead along the course of old Route 66. The story of Route 66 has always been about someone heading west, from the Depression-era family fleeing the Dust Bowl to the World War II–era migrants seeking defense jobs to the 1950s and 1960s family vacations to Disneyland. Along every mile are signs: to mark the way or to make us want to pull over and fill up the tank, stay the night, or pick up a kitschy souvenir.

Illinois was one of two states where the highway was completely paved when Route 66 was commissioned in 1926. But it was a bumpy road to get to that point. At the turn of the twentieth century on the prairie, long-distance travel was primarily by train. The black prairie soil turned into an impassable quagmire when it rained. In October 1903, Miss Pierre Chouteau Scott set a record by driving from St. Louis to Chicago in just fifty-four hours. It would be 1910 before the state licensed motor vehicles, with the resulting funds earmarked for roads.

Within a few years, private associations began marking roads on their own, and the first true road signs along the future Route 66 in Illinois marked the Pontiac Trail, officially known as Route 4. It was named for the chief of the Ottawa tribe and marked in 1915 by the B. F. Goodrich

Above: Because of the one-way streets, the first signs marking the westbound beginning of Route 66 are on the south side of Adams Street west of Michigan Avenue. But purists will complain that Route 66 never really began on Adams. The street only handled westbound traffic starting in 1955. The massive skyscrapers form a canyon. The skyscrapers include architectural landmarks such as the Rookery, the Monadnock Building, and the Chicago Board of Trade. The Willis Tower is the tallest building in the Western Hemisphere. The brave can check out the view from the Skydeck with its clear floor.

Opposite: Neon sign pointing the way to Lexington, Illinois. *Scott E. Nelson/Shutterstock*

Company. The federal government named Route 4 as one of five routes in Illinois eligible for federal funds in 1916.

The state of Illinois passed a bond issue providing for four thousand miles (6,440 kilometers) of "hard roads" in 1918. State Bond Issue (SBI) Route 4 was assigned to the route from Forty-Eighth Street and Ogden Avenue in Cicero to East St. Louis, and it was paved along its entire length by the end of 1923, just in time for the era of the rum runners and the bootleggers who smuggled illegal hooch and shot it out with rivals and the law as the gang wars in the big cities spilled out into the countryside. Meanwhile, overloaded trucks were destroying the roads. In 1921 lawmakers authorized the hiring of eight state highway patrol officers to cover all of Illinois. At first, their main concern was enforcing the weight limits.

At that time, Illinois and Kansas were the only two states where Route 66 was completely paved, and Kansas could only claim thirteen miles (twenty-one kilometers) out of the entire route.

Avery coined the phrase "The Main Street of America" and the US 66 Highway Association publicized the route. A footrace from Los Angeles to New York, dubbed the Bunion Derby, provided the opportunity. A diverse group of 199 runners started from Los Angeles on March 4, 1928, and promoter C. C. "Cash and Carry" Pyle pledged a first prize of $25,000. The men ran in all sorts of conditions, with Pyle pinching pennies on accommodations and food.

Just seventy-two men made it to East St. Louis, Illinois, on April 27. Near Staunton, eccentric runner and actor Lucien Frost was disqualified for riding in the trunk of a car. It cost him a movie deal. In Joliet, the runners cheered when creditors seized Pyle's lavish custom bus. In an effort to save money by forcing more runners to quit, Pyle increased the daily run to fifty-nine miles (ninety-five kilometers). Another twelve men dropped out by the time the runners reached Chicago on May 5. Half-Cherokee runner Andy Payne, from the Route 66 town of Foyil, Oklahoma, won the race, and Route 66 reaped the publicity.

Route 66 was evolving from the day it was commissioned. A new roadway was already under construction across the Des Plaines River from the old Pontiac Trail through Lemont and Lockport. The original route between Springfield and Staunton was bypassed in 1931 in favor of a straighter shot via Litchfield and Mount Olive.

Above: William Mitchell opened his restaurant on Jackson Boulevard in 1923, and his son Lou joined the business in 1935. The restaurant moved to the other side of the street in 1949. Lou Mitchell's is famous for handing out donut holes to waiting customers and a box of Milk Duds candies to the ladies and kids. Lou Mitchell sold the restaurant to his niece in 1992, and it remains in the family.

Route 66 leaves Chicago via Ogden Avenue; it was the best route across a dismal nine-mile swamp, once an important American Indian portage between Lake Michigan and the Des Plaines River but a serious impediment to the growth of Chicago. The road was named for Chicago's first mayor, William Butler Ogden, in 1872.

Opposite: Route 66 began or ended, depending on your point of view, at Jackson Boulevard and Michigan Avenue in front of the Art Institute of Chicago. In 1937 Jackson and Route 66 were extended east to US Highway 41, today's Lakeshore Drive. In 1955, Jackson became a one-way eastbound street between Ogden and Michigan Avenues. Adams Street just to the north would carry westbound traffic west of Michigan, and the eastern terminus remained at Jackson and Lakeshore.

During the Great Depression, images of desperate refugees from the Dust Bowl inspired John Steinbeck to label Route 66 "The Mother Road." But Route 66 brought economic opportunity to Illinois as mom-and-pop cafés, gas stations, and motels sprang up, and government relief programs put men to work improving the roads.

The 1941 Defense Highway Act authorized construction of a modern four-lane limited-access route between Chicago and St. Louis. During World War II, the crushing weight of oversized trucks and heavy equipment left many sections virtually unusable. In some areas, plans called for two new lanes to be constructed and the old lanes abandoned. The abandoned lanes would be rebuilt after the war, creating a four-lane highway.

The postwar years are considered the Golden Age, when Nat King Cole sang "(Get Your Kicks on) Route 66" and Americans hit the road in record numbers. But the popularity of Route 66 also led to its demise, as the old two-lane sections became inadequate. Work continued on four-lane limited-access segments until the entire route between Chicago and St. Louis was four lanes by 1956. Interstate 55 now follows most of the postwar four-lane road. The Route 66 shields came down in Illinois in 1977.

Above: Just down Ogden Avenue, the sign at Henry's Drive-In on Ogden Avenue in Cicero proclaims that the Chicago-style hot dog served traditionally with the fries on top is "A Meal in Itself." Bill Henry began selling hot dogs from a wooden trailer in 1946 and then built a six-stool, red-brick building. When a McDonald's opened nearby in 1960, Henry added a ceramic tile exterior and designed a new sign.

Right: An old stretch of highway takes travelers to the "Nationally Famous Chicken Basket" in Willowbrook and a step back in time. Irv Kolarik took a fried chicken recipe from two local women and opened the "Nationally Famous Chicken Basket" in 1946. To attract business in the winter, Kolarik once flooded the roof and hired ice skaters. Dell Rhea and his wife Grace bought the restaurant in 1963, and their son Patrick took over in 1986.

Cicero is best known as the home of Al Capone, the notorious gangster who apparently stopped at nearly every roadhouse between here and St. Louis. So many places in Illinois claim a connection to Capone that it's a wonder he ever found time for a life of crime.

A landmark since opening in 1960, the Cindy Lyn Motel billed itself as the last motel before the city and has remained in the same family throughout its history. The motel has been featured in the TV shows *Empire, Chicago Fire,* and *Shameless. Cindy Lyn Motel*

Joliet Area Historical Museum

JOLIET US 66

Above: Joliet was originally named Juliet, probably an alternate spelling of the name of explorer Louis Jolliet. The name was changed in 1845. The Joliet Historical Museum is located downtown and has a section devoted to Route 66.

Left: Jack Schore's Texaco Station opened at Dwight in 1933, and Basil "Tubby" Ambler ran it from 1935 to 1965. Phil Becker took over the station in 1970, and it would later be rebranded to Marathon. The station closed in 2006, at which time it was recognized as one of the oldest stations still in operation on Route 66. The restored structure is now a visitor center.

RUBENS

RIALTO

SQUARE

SATURDAY, OCTOBER 5 AT 8PM

FRANK CALIENDO

ED BY MILLER LITE CONCERT SERIES

GREGG

SIAT C

The Rialto Square Theatre mixes several architectural styles with a lobby modeled after the Hall of Mirrors at the Palace of Versailles outside Paris. "The Jewel of Joliet" opened on May 24, 1926, and was restored in 1980.

Near Ellwood are the Abraham Lincoln National Cemetery and the Midewin National Tallgrass Prairie, the largest open space in Illinois. This was once the site of a massive ordnance plant, where forty-eight workers died in an explosion during World War II. Plainfield was known as the "Crossroads of America," because Route 66 intersected with US Highway 30, the famous Lincoln Highway.

GEMINI GIANT

Above: The Gemini Giant served as a marquee for the Launching Pad Drive-In at Wilmington beginning in 1965, the height of the Space Age. Owners John and Bernice Korelc added one of the so-called Muffler Men, twenty-eight-foot-tall fiberglass statues from the International Fiberglass Company, decked out in a helmet and holding a rocket. The giant still greets travelers today, but the Launching Pad closed in 2013.

Right: A signpost marks the turnoff to Odell. When Route 66 ran through town, it was so busy that a tunnel was constructed under the roadway to allow churchgoers and schoolchildren to cross safely. In 1944 a four-lane bypass was constructed a few blocks to the west. The tunnel was no longer needed and was filled in. *Judy Hinckley*

Above left: Patrick O'Connell constructed his Standard Oil station in Odell in 1932. Robert Close bought it in 1967 and operated a body shop there until 1999. The Route 66 Association of Illinois, the Village of Odell, the National Park Service Route 66 Corridor Preservation Program, and other agencies and groups pitched in to restore the structure, which now serves as a visitor center. *Judy Hinckley*

Above: Lester Dill, owner of Meramec Caverns on Route 66 in Stanton, Missouri, had barns for hundreds of miles painted with advertisements for the classic roadside attraction. The Route 66 Association of Illinois Preservation Committee restored this barn at Cayuga, and it is the last one remaining along the route in Illinois. A similar barn in Hamel was destroyed by a storm in 2011.

Left: Pontiac has embraced its Route 66 heritage. The Route 66 Association of Illinois Hall of Fame and Museum is located in the old city hall and fire station. Behind the museum, a mural features a massive 66 shield. The sign at right was salvaged from the Wishing Well Motel in La Grange, Illinois.

Top: On Route 66's original alignment through Chenoa, this advertisement for Selz Royal Blue Shoes was uncovered when the adjacent building was demolished. German immigrant Rolf Selz founded the Selz Shoe Company that once made a pair for Queen Elizabeth. That's when it started using "Royal" in its advertising. The company closed in the 1940s.

Above: A mile-long section of the original Route 66 at Lexington has been preserved and turned into a walking trail with vintage billboards and a set of Burma-Shave signs. The section is opened to auto traffic for special events. *Judy Hinckley*

Left: Many buildings in Pontiac are adorned with murals celebrating the heritage of the community and Route 66. The Walldogs, a group of sign painters, painted many of them. The International Walldog Mural and Sign Art Museum in Pontiac celebrates the history of painted advertising signs on the walls of buildings.

Above: In 1928 J. P. Walters and John Geske founded the Dixie Truckers home at Route 66 and US Highway 136 in McLean. They named it the Dixie to symbolize Southern hospitality. One of the best-known truck stops on Route 66, the original building burned in 1965.

The Dixie was back in business before the ashes of the fire cooled, using one of the cabins moved up to the pumps. C. J. Geske, John Geske's daughter, and her husband Chuck Beeler took over in 1967 and sold in 2003. The Road Ranger chain purchased the Dixie in 2012.

Above right: Ernie Edwards, the owner of the Pig Hip Restaurant in Broadwell, was beloved by Route 66 travelers as the "Old Coot." His restaurant opened in 1937 and got a new name when a customer asked for a "slice of that pig hip." This sign was salvaged when the restaurant burned on March 5, 2007. Edwards passed away in 2012.

Right: Across from the Palm's Grill Café, the Route 66 Park in Atlanta features a display of reinterpretive artwork created by artists using a blank Route 66 shield as a canvas. Sarah Vandenbusch of Burbank, California, painted this particular shield in 2013.

Opposite: Normal is the birthplace of the Steak 'n Shake chain, where the company's motto has always been "In Sight It Must Be Right." Gus Belt opened the original location on Main Street in 1934 and began franchising in 1945.

Burma-Shave Signs

It's clear that an advertising campaign has been successful when folks remember it fifty years after it ended. The last official Burma-Shave signs disappeared from the American roadsides in 1963, but the witty sayings are fondly remembered and are often re-created by the nostalgic among us. The ancestor of today's viral content begins with a smelly liniment.

Clinton Odell of Edina, Minnesota, claimed he got the formula for his product from an old sea captain. It was very effective for relieving pain from burns and apparently also aided in healing. Odell called the noxious goop Burma Vita, because the oils used came from the Malay Peninsula. Vita is the Latin word for "life." But the product wasn't moving very well, because it stunk to high heaven and would only be used by someone who was in serious pain.

Clinton acquired a sample of a British brushless shaving cream called Lloyd's Euxesis and decided he could make a better shaving cream. Odell hired a chemist who tried nearly 300 formulas before going back to an old batch made on the 143rd try. That's when it was discovered that aging the stuff for a couple months resulted in a fine shaving cream, which Clinton dubbed Burma-Shave. Sales remained soft until Clinton's sons Leonard and Alan introduced some innovative ideas.

The first plan they hit on was to sell jars on approval. In other words, the Odell lads would cold call on a potential customer and offer them a jar of Burma-Shave. If the customer liked it, the boys would come back later to collect their fifty cents. If not, the client simply returned the unused portion. This didn't work out very well, and the Odells were nearly broke when Alan remembered some sequential roadside signs they had seen while out pushing the product. At first patriarch Clinton Odell wasn't sold, but Alan convinced him to invest $200 in the idea.

In late 1925, Alan and Leonard bought some secondhand boards, cut them into thirty-six-inch (ninety-one-centimeter) lengths and painted them with advertising slogans. (Initially, they didn't rhyme.) There were six signs to a set, with the sixth always reading "Burma-Shave." Each sign was placed roughly one hundred paces apart and two sets were thrown up quickly on the two US highways serving Minneapolis just in time to beat the hard freeze. Within a few weeks, the orders began coming in, because it turned out that a sequence of signs held the viewer's attention longer. The first rhyming series of signs appeared in 1928, and they were displaying a pithy sense of humor by 1929. Some of those early signs included:

Shaving brushes
You'll soon see 'em
Way down east
In some
Museum
Burma-Shave

Every Shaver
Now can snore

Six more minutes
Than before
By using
Burma-Shave

Are your whiskers
When you wake
Tougher than
A two bit steak?
Try
Burma-Shave

Alan and Leonard traveled the nation looking for flat stretches with unobstructed views and long enough for the entire sequence. They sometimes would knock on a farmer's door, offering free Burma-Shave products and up to $25 per year for the right of way. That $25 went a long way during the Great Depression.

At the height of their popularity, more than seven thousand sets of Burma-Shave signs were along US highways. Burma-Shave signs appeared nearly everywhere, except in Arizona, New Mexico, and Nevada, because there wasn't as much traffic. No one driving in Massachusetts saw them either, because the foliage and winding roads made it difficult to find ideal locations.

Since there needed to be a continuous flow of new messages, the company came up with an annual contest that offered $100 for every verse selected. With up to fifty thousand entries each year, the task was just too large for the Odell family business. They hired professional copywriters to wade through all the entries. In 1935, some

of the signs began featuring safety messages:

Don't lose
Your head
To gain a minute
You need your head
Your brains are in it
Burma-Shave

Keep well
To the right
Of the oncoming car
Get your close shaves
From the half-pound jar
Burma-Shave

Hardly a driver
Is still alive
Who passed
On hills
At 75
Burma-Shave

Don't stick
Your elbow
Out so far
It might go home
In another car
Burma-Shave

They weren't above reminding guys that Burma-Shave might help with the ladies:

She eyed
His beard
And said no dice
The weddings off
I'll cook the rice
Burma-Shave

He had the ring
He had the flat
But she felt his chin
And that
Was that
Burma-Shave

The firm had some close shaves when it came to promotions. Consumers worked themselves into a lather when Burma-Shave signs decided to poke a little fun at the coupon craze.

Free Offer! Free Offer!
Rip a fender
From your car
Mail it for
A half-pound jar
Burma-Shave

Most folks realized it was just a joke. But some decided to hold the makers of Burma-Shave to their word. No one ripped the fenders off their own cars, but they made a trip to the local junkyard, picked out one that was nicely dented and rusty, and shipped it in. A few creative individuals mailed in

fenders from toy cars. Everyone who sent in a fender, large or small, shiny or rusty, received a half-pound jar, and Burma-Shave reaped a ton of publicity.

Burma-Shave had another brush with disaster in 1955. Comic Fred Allen on his radio show did a parody of the Burma-Shave signs:

> Free! Free!
>> A trip
>>> To Mars
>>>> For 900
>>>>> Empty jars
>>>>> *Burma-Shave*

The company thought it was pretty safe with that one. Who on Earth could come up with nine hundred empty jars?

It underestimated the manager of the Red Owl supermarket in Appleton, Wisconsin. Arliss "Frenchie" French put on a full-fledged promotional extravaganza at the store, complete with a kid-sized rocket ship, and placed an ad in the local paper under the headline "Send Frenchie to Mars." The ad offered fifteen cents for each empty Burma-Shave container. As the pile of empties in the store began to grow, French wrote the company asking where he should ship the jars. He received a playful reply: "If a trip to Mars you'd earn, remember friend, there's no return."

French fired back in style: "Let's not quibble, let's not fret, Gather your forces, I'm all set." Another telegram arrived in Appleton. This time it read: "Our rockets are ready, We ain't just splitting hairs, Just send us the jars, And arrange your affairs." Now the executives were sweating. The general manager of Burma-Shave at first thought of sending French to the Mars Candy Company in Chicago. Then a Hollywood publicist hired by the supermarket chain came up with a better idea. French was offered a trip to the tiny hamlet of Moers, Germany. With a straight face, it was announced that the name of the town was pronounced "Mars."

Everyone played along with the joke, and when French arrived at Burma-Shave's head office on December 2, 1958, he was ready to go. He sported a football helmet on his head and was clad in a silvery "space suit" with a Red Owl stores logo. Burma-Shave hired an armored car to deliver the empties.

The press lapped it up as Burma-Shave execs handed over the plane tickets and some Burma-Shave to "barter with the natives." French remained decked out in his outfit as he arrived at the airport in Düsseldorf with his wife. The entire population of Moers, all seventy-eight residents, came out to greet them. Once again, the publicity for Burma-Shave was worth far more than the expense of the trip.

Even as Burma-Shave basked in the glow of the publicity, the signs were becoming obsolete. As speeds increased, the signs had to be spaced farther apart and were harder to read. And an interstate highway is no place for casual reading. Sales of Burma-Shave peaked in 1947 and then began to decline as the product and its advertising was seen as old-fashioned. Burma-Vita was sold in February 1963 and the brand became part of Phillip Morris, which decided that advertising on television was more effective. The signs were removed from the roadways just before the Highway Beautification Act of 1965 would have mandated their removal anyway.

It's been more than fifty years since anyone has seen a Burma-Shave sign in the wild, but they are not gone entirely. A set resides in the Smithsonian in Washington, DC, and at the Henry Ford Museum in Michigan. Replica signs can be found along Route 66 along the Memory Lane Section at Lexington, Illinois, west of Seligman, Arizona, and at the Hackberry Store in Hackberry, Arizona.

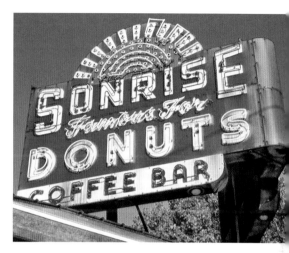

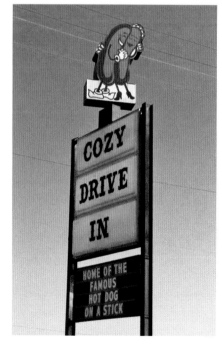

Above: There are some sights to see along the post-1930 alignment, which often serves as a humble service road. Some parts of the old four-lane are still there, one-half abandoned years ago, leaving behind a two-lane road and two lanes being reclaimed by nature. The Route 66 Association of Illinois restored the Art's Motel sign in 2007, but the restaurant and motel at Farmersville are now closed.

Above right: In 1930 Route 66 was shifted to enter Springfield on Peoria Road. Bill Shea's old gas station turned mini museum was a must-see here. Route 66 then followed Ninth Street and Sixth Streets. This alignment became City 66 in 1940, when the bypass opened.

   Sonrise Donuts has passed into history, but the beautiful sign erected in 1956 remains atop the building on Ninth Street.

Right: The Cozy Dog is probably the best-known spot on Route 66 in Springfield and is said to be the birthplace of the corn dog. Ed Waldmire Jr. opened the Cozy Dog Drive In on September 27, 1950. Ed Waldmire's son, Bob, was an iconic Route 66 artist and his artwork adorns the restaurant. The Cozy Dog moved just up the road to its current location in 1996.

Top: The Shrine of Our Lady of the Highways has watched over travelers on a farm near Raymond since 1959. Frances Marten donated the site on his farm, and local Catholic youths erected the shrine.

Above left: The pre- and post-1930 alignments of Route 66 meet near Hamel and follow today's Illinois Route 157.

Above: Edwardsville is the third-oldest city in Illinois and is named for territorial governor Ninian Edwards. It was the home of the famous Cathcart's Café and boasts an attractive downtown highlighted by the Wildey Theatre, opened in 1909. The Wildey closed in 1984 but was restored after the City of Edwardsville took over in 1999.

Left: In 1924, Greek immigrant Pete Adam opened the Ariston Café in Carlinville. The name is from the Greek *aristos*, or "the best." The restaurant was moved to Litchfield after Route 66 was relocated, and this landmark opened in July 1935. Pete's son Nick and Nick's wife, Demi, took over in 1966, and the restaurant is still in the family.

Above right: Vintage Shell signage can still be seen at Soulsby Shell in Mount Olive. Henry Soulsby and his son Russell opened the station in 1926. Russell ran the station with his sister Ola until 1993. The Soulsby Station Society and owner Mike Dragovich maintain the site today for Route 66 travelers.

Top: Beginning in 1936, Route 66 passed through Mitchell on the way to the Chain of Rocks Bridge over the Mississippi. The Bel-Air Drive-In at Mitchell opened in April 1954 and closed in 1987. Only the battered marquee remains.

Above: Vic Suhling built his station across from the Ariston in 1957. It later became a Deep Rock Station but was demolished in 1990, leaving the forlorn sign standing alone. The Litchfield Museum and Route 66 Welcome Center opened here in 2011, and the sign was restored in 2013.

Left: Herman Raffaelle opened the Luna Café in Mitchell on September 1, 1932. Legend said that the cherry in the glass on the neon marquee was lit when "ladies were available" and that the Luna was a hangout for Al Capone. But restoration of the sign in 2012 revealed that the cherry could not be lit separately. Larry Wofford operates the landmark today.

Rest Haven
COURT

LOW RATES
CK PARKING
HBD

Chapter 2

Show Me 66

Missouri is the birthplace of Route 66, and the Show Me State has plenty to show the Mother Road traveler. The state presents amazing changes in scenery from the Mississippi River to the forested hills and pristine streams of the Ozarks. The signs feature Jesse James hideouts, Walnut Bowls, stereotypical hillbillies, and Missouri mules.

The Osage first blazed footpaths atop a ridge that ran between the Ozarks and the confluence of the Missouri and Mississippi Rivers. Cherokee forced to move from the southeastern United States to Oklahoma made the bitter journey on the "Trail of Tears" along part of this route in the 1830s. In 1837 the state authorized a road between St. Louis and Springfield following the Kickapoo Trail or Osage Trail.

When the telegraph arrived, the stage route between St. Louis and Springfield became known as the Wire Road. The Blue and the Gray marched along its dusty path to battle at Carthage and Wilson's Creek. By the 1880s, resorts were springing up along the Gasconade and Big Piney Rivers serviced by the Frisco Railroad. They were a popular destination for sportsmen from the big cities, but the Ozarks were still inaccessible to the masses.

The first automobiles came to Missouri in 1891, and more than sixteen thousand were registered by 1911. C. H. Laessig opened the first gas station in the United States at 412 Theresa Street in St. Louis in 1905. In 1919 AAA opened a tourist camp in St. Louis's Forest Park. Early

Above: Rising 630 feet (192 meters) above the Mississippi River, the Gateway Arch is our nation's tallest national monument. The last piece was put in place on October 28, 1965, and the entire grounds were renovated and reconfigured in 2015. Note the sign directing traffic west on 66, today's Interstate 44.

Opposite: The Rest Haven Court Motel sign in Springfield, Missouri. *Steve Lagreca/Shutterstock*

33

Original Route 66 crossed the Mississippi on the McKinley Bridge and passed Crown Candy Kitchen on St. Louis Avenue. Greek confectioners Harry Karandzieff and his best friend Pete Jugaloff opened Crown Candy in 1913. Karandzieff's son George took the business over in the 1950s and his sons, Andy, Tommy, and Mike, run the business today, with a fourth generation pitching in. Crown Candy is known for its own confections, vintage Coca-Cola memorabilia, and a heart-stopping BLT sandwich.

The original route eventually wound west and south to end up on Manchester Road. Now State Highway 100, Manchester was intended as a temporary route until a new highway was completed through Pacific to Gray Summit.

motorists didn't care for the finery of the big city hotels. Many derided as "tin can tourists" just camped beside the road where they pleased.

As in other states, promoters of the private trails were weaving a tangled web across Missouri. They gave their road an important-sounding name such as the Ozark Trails Route, or Jefferson Highway, and painted color-coded stripes on fence posts, telegraph poles, or any handy surface. Drivers followed the colors to travel the Lincoln Highway, the Dixie Highway, or the Old Spanish Trail. In 1917 The Ozark Trail Association mapped out a system of routes between St. Louis and Romeroville, New Mexico. From there, the Ozark Trail Route joined the National Old Trails Road to Los Angeles. By 1918 a segment of the Ozark Trail was paved from Webb City through Joplin to the Kansas state line.

The early highway associations made money from "contributions" by merchants to have the highway routed past their business. Drivers were often taken miles out of their way. Missouri voters took action in 1920, approving a $60 million road bond issue for a state road system to "Lift Missouri Out of the Mud." In August 1922, the State Highway Commission designated routes connecting the big cities. The road between St. Louis and Joplin was designated as State Highway 14.

In 1925 meeting at the Jefferson Hotel in St. Louis, the American Association of State Highway Officials approved a numbering system for the proposed federal highways. A lengthy dispute over the number for the route from Chicago to Los Angeles was settled only when Missouri and Oklahoma officials met in Springfield on April 30, 1926, and noticed that the catchy sounding "66" was still available—thus allowing Springfield to claim it is the birthplace of Route 66.

John T. Woodruff was a Springfield civic leader and owner of the Kentwood Arms Hotel. He was someone whom Cyrus Avery had known in the Ozark Trails Association. Avery and Woodruff invited representatives from all of the eight Route 66 states to Springfield on February 4, 1927. That day Woodruff became the first president of the Route 66 Association, which coined the phrase "The Main Street of America."

The runners in the Bunion Derby transcontinental footrace entered Missouri on April 21, 1928. When negotiations for payments to have the race stop in Carthage failed, promoter C. C. Pyle opted for Miller instead. Angry residents of Carthage pelted the lead cars with eggs. The runners made it to St. Louis on April 29. The city refused to pay for the race to stop there, so the runners stayed on a hillside inn west of the city.

In 1928 the Pierce Oil Company of St. Louis began erecting lavish facilities about 125 miles (201 kilometers) apart with accommodations that rivaled anything in the big cities. Pierce also pioneered the use of road maps and even erected signs guiding those intrepid automobilists, all the while promoting the Ozarks to the masses as a tourist wonderland.

Missouri was the third state to completely pave 66 within its borders. The final section was completed on January 5, 1931, in Phelps County near Arlington.

World War II brought even more traffic, and the first four-lane divided section was constructed to serve Fort Leonard Wood in 1943. It included

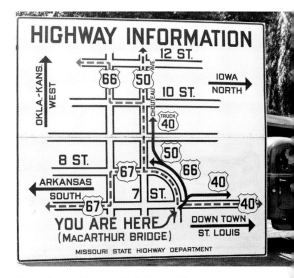

The southern or historic route is the most famous path through the St. Louis area, although it was designated only as City 66 during most of the Route 66 era. From the Municipal/MacArthur Bridge, 66 headed west on Chouteau to Twelfth, Gravois, Chippewa, and Watson. This bewildering sign stood at the west end of the MacArthur Bridge.

Top: In 1936 the mainline of 66 shifted to the Chain of Rocks Bridge over the Mississippi north of the city. The route via Chouteau, Twelfth, Gravois, and Chippewa was designated as City 66. The Chain of Rocks Bridge is now one of the longest pedestrian and bicycle bridges in the world. The 66 Motel sign is modeled after one that actually stood on the Watson Road alignment west of the city limits. *Library of Congress*

Above: In 1929, 66 shifted to the Municipal or Free Bridge, renamed in honor of General Douglas MacArthur in 1942. With some variations, 66 followed Chouteau, Manchester, Boyle, and Clayton Avenues through Forest Park before picking up McCausland and turning west on Manchester. A vintage Coca-Cola sign still adorns the Eat-Rite Diner on Chouteau while another advertises six hamburgers for $5.10.

Right: The Grove is a growing and lively district along Manchester Road between Kingshighway and Vandeventer in St. Louis. Within just a few years, this part of the Tower Grove neighborhood has been transformed into a diverse mix of restaurants, nightclubs, and retail.

the largest highway cut on a US highway at the time, blasting through the solid rock near Hooker. Many of those soldiers who served at "Fort Lost in the Woods" would return with their families to vacation in the Ozarks after the war, the glory years of Route 66. Roadside hucksterism was at its height. The signs became more lavish as establishments tried hard to set themselves apart from the competition.

As the traffic counts and speeds got higher, so did the toll from accidents along "Bloody 66." The road became a victim of its own success. On August 2, 1956, Missouri became the first state to award a contract under the new law, for work on four-lane Route 66 in Laclede County. The nation's first actual interstate construction took place west of the Missouri River on Interstate 70 at St. Charles.

Missouri wasn't giving up on 66 just yet. In December 1962, the state petitioned federal officials to designate the route between Chicago and Los Angeles as Interstate 66. The feds refused. The towns along Route 66 between Carthage and Springfield threatened to sue to keep the US 66 designation and highway officials responded by building Interstate 44 farther south. By 1965, those towns were completely bypassed. By 1972, I-44 had replaced 66 across Missouri. Finally, in June 1974, officials of the American Association of State Highway and Transportation voted to eliminate US Route 66 from Chicago to Joplin. The last Route 66 signs in Missouri remained up until January 24, 1977, when Interstate 55 in Illinois was brought up to standards.

I-44 replaced old 66 in Missouri, but it couldn't kill it. Drivers continued to go out of their way to connect with the people and travel through the heart of the towns instead of around them. By 1990, there was enough interest to form the Route 66 Association of Missouri "to preserve, promote, and develop old Route 66 in Missouri." Today, the association and Route 66 "roadies" are dedicated to preserving the road for future generations.

For Route 66 to become the road west, it had to pass through St. Louis. After all, the city was the start of the great westward migrations of the 1800s and its most famous landmark is a monument to those who kept going west. By the Route 66 era, St. Louis had turned its back on the riverfront. The area was filled with grimy tenements and warehouses. Work started to clear the buildings for the riverfront memorial in 1939. But funding problems and haggling delayed construction for more than two decades.

Top: No visit to St. Louis is complete without a stop at Ted Drewes Frozen Custard, opened in 1941. The treat is best eaten as a "concrete," basically a shake so thick you can turn it upside down. In the winter, Ted Drewes Jr. converts the stand into a lot selling Christmas trees. In 1955 Route 66 moved to the Veteran's (now ML King) Bridge to the Third Street Expressway (Interstate 55) to the city route at Gravois. When 66 moved to the Poplar Street Bridge in 1967, the mainline came back to Gravois, Chippewa, and Watson. Those signs came down in February 1975, and 66 shifted to Interstate 44 until decertification in 1977.

Above: The streamlined Coral Court Motel on Watson Road was one of the finest on Route 66 and opened in 1941. Late in its life, it gained a racy reputation due to an association with a notorious kidnapping and because the rooms with private garages could be rented for four to eight hours, a service originally intended to allow truckers to rest. Despite an intense preservation effort, it was demolished in 1995, and a subdivision stands on the site today.

Left: From 1936 to 1955, Mainline Route 66 from the Chain of Rocks Bridge followed present-day Dunn Road and turned south on Lindbergh Boulevard through Kirkwood. This route was designated as By-Pass 66 from 1955 to 1965. Spencer's Grill in the heart of Kirkwood opened on October 14, 1947. William Spencer and his wife Irene kept it open twenty-four hours per day, making the most of the Route 66 traffic. The grill was remodeled in 1948, and the neon sign and clock shown here were installed at that time. Kirkwood was established in 1853 and was the first planned community west of the Mississippi.

Jump on Interstate 44 for a short distance to the Route 66 State Park on the former site of the community of Times Beach. The town, on, and sometimes in, the Meramec River, was founded in 1925 when the *St. Louis Star-Times* offered a 20- by 100-foot lot for $67.50 with a subscription. Waste oil was sprayed on the dusty streets in the 1970s. After a disastrous flood in December 1982, residents learned the oil was tainted with dioxin. The Environmental Protection Agency leveled the town and the dioxin-contaminated soil was burned in a controversial incinerator. Route 66 State Park opened on the cleaned-up site in 1999.

The bluffs along 66 through Pacific are riddled with caves created by silica mining and a Route 66–era scenic overlook on the bluff is now a park. In 1934, former bootleggers and brothers James and William Smith opened the Red Cedar Tavern in Pacific, built with red cedar logs. James Smith Jr. took over and hired Katherine Brinkman as a waitress. They married in 1940 and the business remained in the family until closing in March 2005. *Jim Thole*

Left: The wonderful porcelain neon sign at the Sunset Motel near Villa Ridge was dark for about thirty years before the Route 66 Corridor Preservation Program and "Team Neon" of the Route 66 Association of Missouri got involved. The Lovelace family opened the motel in 1946. Lolita and Oliver Krueger ran the Sunset from 1971 to 2006, and it is still in the family.

Several abandoned businesses line the route (now Route AT) as it descends into the valley of the Bourbeuse River. There were once so many gas stations, cafés, and motels here that the highway was labeled as the "Million Dollar Stretch." Across the river, it unites with US Highway 50 for 6.5 miles (ten kilometers), slowly climbing out of the valley. *Jim Thole*

Opposite: The Donut Drive-In on Chippewa Street opened in 1952. There was no drive-up window. "Drive-In" simply meant off-street parking was available. With help from a National Park Service Route 66 Corridor Preservation Grant and the Neon Preservation Committee of the Route 66 Association of Missouri, the sign with its animated dropping red neon donuts was restored in 2008.

Rest Stop

Meramec Caverns

Anyone who has driven on Route 66 or Interstate 44 in Missouri has seen them. The billboards and painted barns for hundreds of miles promote "The Greatest Show under the Earth" at Meramec Caverns near Stanton. The signs and the barns are just part of the story.

Roughly 400 million years ago, Meramec Caverns began to form when groundwater began seeping into the dolomite and limestone bedrock beneath the Missouri Ozarks. Erosion created a seven-level cave system with twenty-six total miles (forty-two kilometers) of known passages and chambers as well as an underground river. The Osage told tales of walls lined with gold.

In 1720, Philip Renault came to southeast Missouri with two hundred men and several hundred slaves to search for lead. Renault had heard the legends and hoped to find gold at the cave. There was no gold, but he found the caverns contained saltpeter, an important ingredient in the manufacturing of gunpowder. An underground gunpowder mill was set up at the Saltpeter Cave prior to the Civil War. It was destroyed when Confederate General Sterling Price and his force of twelve thousand men invaded Missouri in September 1864. That raid gave birth to the cave's best-known legend.

Decades later, cave promoter Lester Dill would claim that future outlaws Jesse and Frank James accompanied the notorious guerilla William Clarke Quantrill on that raid. According to Dill, Jesse James became familiar with the passages and later used that knowledge when he turned to a life of crime, eluding a posse by escaping through a hidden passage. It makes for a good story anyway.

A dance floor was constructed in the cave during the 1890s, and nearly every weekend during the summer, music filled the 60-degree air. The Frisco Railroad brought even more revelers.

As a youngster, Lester B. Dill began picking up extra change by leading tours of Fisher's Cave, just up the Meramec River from Saltpeter Cave. Dill's father, Thomas Benton Dill, had the original vision for Meramec State Park and worked tirelessly for its establishment. He served as the first park superintendent from 1927 to 1933. When his father's cave concession expired, the younger Dill set out to find another one.

He didn't have to go far. Saltpeter Cave was just outside the boundaries of the state park. Lester leased the cave on May 1, 1933. There were already three commercial caves nearby, Onondaga Cave, Missouri Caverns, and Cathedral Cave, so many of the locals were convinced that Dill had cave bats in his belfry.

The cave opened on Memorial Day 1933 and six people paid forty cents for the tour. There wasn't time to build a parking lot, but Dill realized the cave entrance could hold two hundred vehicles and promoted Meramec Caverns as the world's "first drive-in cave."

Dill brought back a form of advertising he had first used at Fisher's Cave in 1928. The family and local youths were kept busy wiring cardboard bumper signs promoting the cave on visitors' vehicles. Although the adhesive had not been developed, Dill had invented the bumper sticker.

The Dills scraped together enough money to buy the cave in 1934. When World War II began, he had another ingenious idea. Saying that more than

Barn near St. Clair, Missouri.

159,000 people could "bed down" in the caverns at one time, he began promoting the cave as the "World's Largest Bomb Shelter." As the Cold War paranoia reached its peak, visitors were given a free "Bomb Shelter Pass," to supposedly use when the nukes fell. It made for good newspaper copy.

Dill also hit on another unique promotion idea that changed the scenery on Route 66. While on their way to Florida for a vacation, Dill and his wife Mary saw an ad for Rock City painted on an old barn. Dill started traveling the road to offer farmers a free paint job on their barn in return for space promoting Meramec Caverns. He also often threw in a pocket watch, a box of chocolates, and lifetime passes to Meramec Caverns. Eventually, there were 350 barns across fourteen states. From 1956 until 2011, Jim Gauer painted every one of them.

In 1942, Dill bought some rusty old pistols and a battered strong box at auction, which were soon "discovered" in the cave near a flat-topped formation. He said it was clear evidence that the James gang had been in the cave and promptly dubbed the formation Loot Rock, where the gang supposedly divided up its ill-gotten gains. The stage was set for the strangest chapter in the history of Meramec Caverns.

By 1948, Dill's son-in-law Rudy Turilli had taken over promotion of the cave. Turilli read with excitement as the newspapers trumpeted that a 102-year-old Lawton, Oklahoma, man using the name J. Frank Dalton claimed he was Jesse

James. Dalton said the man killed on April 3, 1882, in St. Joseph was actually two-bit outlaw Charlie Bigelow.

Sensing a publicity gold mine, Turilli convinced the alleged outlaw to come to Meramec Caverns and stay in a cabin at the cave. Meramec Caverns was in the headlines all over the world on March 10, 1950, when Turilli brought J. Frank Dalton to the Franklin County, Missouri, courthouse in Union and asked a judge to legally change Dalton's name to Jesse Woodson James. Judge Ransom Breuer ruled that if Dalton was Jesse James, he had never changed his name to begin with.

Dalton died at the age of 103 in Granbury, Texas. His tombstone bears the name Jesse James. But Turilli wouldn't let the legend die. In 1964, he opened the Jesse James Museum as an addition to Snell's Restaurant on Route 66 in Sullivan. A year later, he moved the museum to Stanton. He installed exhibits with bizarre wax figures, framed autopsy photos, and artifacts to present his case to tourists.

In 1995, the legends were supposedly laid to rest when the body buried under the name Jesse James in a Kearney, Missouri, cemetery was exhumed and the DNA evidence indicated it was indeed the body of the notorious bad man. To this day, some people don't believe it.

In the 1960s, the Art Linkletter TV show *People Are Funny* put a newlywed couple in a small nook at the caverns and dressed them up as cave people. They were promised a honeymoon in

Jesse and Frank James guard their loot at the entrance to Meramec Caverns.

the Bahamas if they found a key hidden in the cranny within ten days. They spent the entire ten days acting out humiliating skits for the tour groups before Dill hid the key.

The Highway Beautification Act of 1965 put the Meramec Cavern barns on the road to oblivion. The barns already in place were allowed to stay and could be repainted, but no new barn signs would be allowed. Only a few examples of barn advertising remain, but somehow the billboards are bigger than ever.

Lester B. Dill fought successfully for legislation protecting Missouri's caves and died on August 13, 1980. His grandson, Lester Turilli Sr., owns the cave today. Some modern touches, including a zip line, have been added. But Meramec Caverns still has a feel of a classic Ozarks Route 66 roadside attraction, complete with a good legend.

Opposite top: The section of 66 between St. Louis and the Shaw Arboretum in Gray Summit was lined with flowers and trees and designated as the Henry Shaw Gardenway in honor of the founder of the Missouri Botanical Garden. Louis Eckelcamp built the Gardenway Motel in 1945. This landmark with its classic glass block sign closed in 2014. *Jim Thole*

Opposite far left: The route then crosses I-44 and past the deteriorating structure that once housed the Diamonds, billed as "The World's Largest Roadside Restaurant." A new incarnation of the Diamonds and a motel was constructed across from the Gardenway Motel after I-44 opened. This incarnation of the Diamonds Restaurant closed in September 2006.

Opposite bottom right: The Skylark Motel in St. Clair was built about 1955 by Charlie Johnson and his son Robert Charles on the new highway west of town. They formerly ran the Johnson's Mo-Tel (also known for a time as Art's) in St. Clair. Note the distinctive pillar with glass block insets on the front of the building, which is now the VFW hall. The neon scene was restored in 2015 with help from the Route 66 Association of Missouri and the National Park Service. *Jim Thole*

Top right: Bob Mullen has accumulated a huge collection of gasoline pumps, service station signs, neon clocks, and thousands of die-cast toys on display at Bob's Gasoline Alley on the fringes of Cuba. The collection can be viewed by appointment. *Judy Hinckley*

Above right: This sign proclaiming "Jesus King of the Road" once hung outside the Jesus Christ Foundation in Cuba. It was moved to a vacant lot just to the east when the foundation relocated in 2003. Folks here in the Bible Belt might point out that 66 is the number of books in the Bible.

Right: West of Rolla, the most scenic stretch of Route 66 in the state begins at the Martin Springs Road exit, leading toward a dead-end section of Old 66 and abandoned Interstate 44. The signs at Vernelle's Motel reflect the highway realignments that have left the place virtually invisible from the interstate. The 1950s sign at the bottom is from when Route 66 ran right in front. When the interstate came through in 1967, the top sign was added. Interstate 44 was relocated in 2006.

Above: Fanning is home of the Route 66 Outpost and the giant Route 66 Red Rocker. It stands over forty-two feet (thirteen meters) tall, measures twenty feet (six meters) across, and weighs 27,500 pounds (12,485 kilograms). The rockers are each over thirty-one feet (nine meters) long. Due to safety concerns, the chair no longer actually rocks.

Above right: The Stony Dell Resort past Arlington once included a hotel, cabins, a goldfish pond, and an enormous swimming pool surrounded by fanciful stonework and fed by an artesian well. It was one of the busiest spots on Route 66: police regularly had to direct traffic. The pool was demolished for construction of Interstate 44 in 1967. The ruins of a few cabins and the abandoned Granny's Ol' Fashioned Cookin' Restaurant remain on the north side of the road.

Right: The road crosses Interstate 44 at Exit 169 and becomes County Z. This area was dubbed Basketville, for the hand-weaved baskets sold by the locals. This section was bypassed by the World War II-era four-lane. But the 1920s route is still there, turning left at the bottom of the cut. The Elbow Inn is on the old road, where a collection of bras from patrons hangs from the ceiling.

Above: A historic byway sign marks the old road approaching the 1923 truss bridge over the Big Piney at Devils Elbow. The bridge was bypassed during World War II and restored in 2014. The State Planning Commission in 1941 named Devils Elbow one of the Seven Beauty Spots of Missouri. Frustrated lumberjacks trying to float tie rafts around a sharp bend in the river named this area.

Originally, Route 66 continued straight north from where the Devils Elbow alignment meets the 1943 four-lane to pass through Morgan Heights. Continuing west on Route Z takes us to St. Robert and the entrance to Fort Leonard Wood. After the fort was built in 1940, a string of bars and other businesses eager to serve the soldiers sprang up at the turnoff from Route 66. Fort Leonard Wood is now home to the US Army Engineer: Chemical, Biological, Radiological and Nuclear and Military Police Schools.

Above right: In Springfield, a left onto Glenstone Avenue keeps travelers on the historic route. Straight on Kearney Street is the bypass route. The Rail Haven Cottage Cabins opened in 1938 at Glenstone Avenue and St. Louis Street. Lawrence Lippman built the cabins with his brother Elwyn in 1938. It was expanded and became the Rail Haven Motel in 1954. Gordon Elliott revived the fading motel in 1994. It is now the nostalgic, yet thoroughly modern, ninety-three-unit Best Western Route 66 Rail Haven.

Above: Newlyweds Emis and Lois Spears and Emis's parents opened Camp Joy at Lebanon in 1927. The other side of this archway at the exit proclaimed: "Teach your baby to say Camp Joy." A young Bob Hope spent the night here and later said he regretted leaving without paying his fifty cents. The Spears family ran the camp until 1971, and a few of the cabins still stand.

Above: The City Route turns west onto St. Louis Avenue. The first Steak 'n Shake Restaurant was located on Route 66 in Normal, Illinois, and opened in 1934. The best-preserved example on Route 66 is at St. Louis Street and North National Avenue in Springfield, little changed since it opened in 1962. *Jim Thole*

Above left: The Graystone Heights Modern Cabins sign is a restoration success story. Graystone Heights opened in 1935 but closed after Interstate 44 bypassed the location west of Springfield. R & S Floral took over the complex in 1963. Present R & S owners John and Alexa Schweke have restored much of the complex and used their own funds to restore the faded old sign. *Jim Thole*

Left: Jessie and Pete Hudson ran the Munger-Moss Sandwich Shop at Devils Elbow and moved the business to Lebanon after being bypassed. They added a motel next to their Munger Moss Restaurant in 1946. The famous sign was added in 1950. Ramona and Bob Lehmann have operated the motel since 1971, and several rooms are decorated in Route 66 themes.

Above right: At Paris Springs, Fred Mason established a garage, café, and cabins he named Gay Parita, after his wife. Mrs. Mason died in 1953, and Fred didn't rebuild after the station burned in 1955. Gary and Fred Turner built this replica, complete with vintage signage, in 2007.

Right: M. E. Gillioz wanted to locate his theater on the proposed Route 66 in Springfield but was unable to find a suitable location. So he bought a building one block away, leased a twenty-foot frontage on St. Louis Street (Route 66), and connected it to the building he owned. Elvis Presley watched a movie here before his 1956 concert. The Gillioz closed in 1980 but was restored and reopened in 2006. The City Route 66 alignment travels around the Public Square, scene of the first Wild West–style shootout. Wild Bill Hickok killed Dave Tutt in a duel over a gambling debt on the square in 1865.

Far right: In 1939, Arthur and Ida Boots opened their motel at the junction of US Highways 66 and 71 in Carthage. Clark Gable once stayed in Room 6. In 2003, The Boots was nearly torn down for a Walgreens. But the deal fell apart amid an outcry from preservationists. Sisters Deborah Harvey and Priscilla Bledsaw rescued the motor court.

Above: Joining State Highway 96, ghostly ruins continue to line the highway in Jasper County, past what's left of Heatonville, Albatross, Phelps, Rescue, Plew, and Avilla. Stay with Highway 96 west to County Road 130 and head north to Red Oak II. Folk artist Lowell Davis moved several old buildings to the site and re-created the "town."

Left: Because Kansas was a dry state until 1948, plenty of rowdy nightclubs and bars were just on the Missouri side of the line. The State Line Mercantile was the first stop for package liquor inside Missouri. The Paddoc family took over the mercantile in 1979, and it is still in operation today.

Top: In Carthage, turning south on Garrison and west on Oak leads to the 66 Drive-In. It's the only survivor of the six drive-in movie theaters that once bore the 66 name. The drive-in opened in 1948 and became a salvage yard in 1985. Mark Goodman cleaned it up, and the restored drive-in opened on April 3, 1997.

Left: Jay Wilder ran a drug store at 224 Main in Joplin and then opened his restaurant at 1216 Main. In 1946, he completed a $50,000 renovation that added a forty-foot-long mahogany bar. There was once an illegal gambling operation upstairs. Clarence Burgraff bought the restaurant in 1977 and sold to Mike and Marsha Pawlus in 1996.

Many of the motels in Joplin offered information about the famous "Spook Light." The strange bouncing light has been appearing in the Tri-State area since the Quapaw Indian days. No one has been able to find an explanation. Headed west, the route is marked as State Highway 66 and makes a beeline straight for the Kansas state line. At a sign marked "Old 66 Next Right" is the turnoff to the original route to Kansas.

Chapter 3

Sunflowers by 66

Only 13.2 miles of Route 66 are in Kansas. When Bobby Troup wrote "(Get Your Kicks on) Route 66," he didn't even mention the state. But Route 66 in Kansas packs in as much history and adventure per mile as any other state. The entire road is still there and can be driven without encountering a single mile of interstate.

Chief Black Dog of the Osage created the first improved road in the region, a trail connecting the villages and hunting grounds between present-day Baxter Springs and Arkansas City, Arkansas. The trail was said to be wide enough for thirty horses to pass abreast.

When an 1836 treaty forced the Cherokee Nation from the southeastern United States, all of what is now Cherokee County was designated as the Cherokee Neutral Lands, designed as a buffer between Missouri and the lands of the Osage. The area was closed to white settlers, but the Reverend John Baxter came anyway in 1849. He built a trading post and inn at the springs on the Military Road connecting Fort Leavenworth with Fort Gibson in the Indian Territory. Baxter was killed by another illegal settler in a land dispute, but his name lived on.

During the Civil War, a small fort was established at Baxter Springs and rebel guerillas led by William Quantrill attacked on October 6, 1863. They were driven back but ambushed a military wagon train and massacred more than one hundred men, mostly in cold blood as they tried to surrender.

Above: This Kansas Historic Route 66 Byway sign is the first indication that one is now traveling the 13.2 miles (21 kilometers) of Mother Road in the state. The Kansas Byways Program was formed to identify and designate scenic roadways for the enjoyment of the traveling public in Kansas.

Opposite: Decorative signs with a Route 66 shield are posted along Main Street in Galena.

51

Right: This sign welcomes tourists to Galena today. It was once a wild mining boomtown where the Main Street between Galena and its rival Empire City was once known as "Red Hot Street." By 1900, the population stood at almost thirty thousand people, and the road that would one day bear the 66 shields became an important link between the mines. Good roads were necessary to carry the heavy mining equipment, and the route between Galena and Riverton was paved in 1924. However the roughly mile-and-a-half of pavement between the east side of Galena and the state line was not completed until September 1927, due in part to delays in acquiring right of way and overcoming major opposition.

Below: The journey continues past the Eagle-Picher smelter. Route 66 shields are painted on the road as it crosses Hell's Half-Acre, where the land bears the scars of decades of mining. The mines left behind a legacy of sinkholes, chat piles, and dangerous heavy metals here. Cleanup work began in the late 1980s, and the vegetation is slowly returning. But the land can't be developed, due to collapsing mineshafts. Blood was also shed here, during labor unrest between 1935 and 1937. The road then crosses the 1927 viaduct over the railroad tracks and makes a left onto the Main Street of Galena.

The cattlemen and cowboys came after the war. Since it was on the border with the Indian Territory, Baxter Springs found itself at the end of the Eastern Shawnee Trail. "The First Cowtown in Kansas" was a wild and practically lawless place until the cattle drives moved on.

The boom came in February 1877. Two boys digging for worms discovered a major deposit of lead ore along Short Creek, north of Baxter Springs. Within months, ten thousand people descended on the area and the Empire Town Company and the Galena Town Company had established rival town sites on opposite sides of the creek. The two towns were incorporated a day apart in June 1877.

"Red Hot Street" connecting Empire City and Galena was known for gambling, prostitution, public drunkenness, and violent death. The competition between the towns heated up in 1877, when Empire City went so far as to erect a stockade to stop travel between the rivals. The townspeople of Galena burned it down and Empire City became part of Galena in 1907.

But the demand for lead had dropped sharply after World War I and jobs became scarce. In 1935, violence swept Galena when miners tried to form a union. Governor Alf Landon declared martial law and sent in the Kansas National Guard.

A restored station with vintage Kan-O-Tex signage brightens the scene where Route 66 turns left into Galena. Melba Rigg, Betty Courtney, Judy Courtney, and Renee Charles launched a revival in Galena when they restored the station, now known as Cars on the Route. The vehicles parked outside include the rusty 1951 International boom truck that inspired the character Tow Mater in the Pixar film *Cars*.

Top: Ghost signs advertising businesses of long ago remain on the side of the old Front Street Garage, directly across the street from Cars on the Route in Galena. The building dates to 1896 and the new owner plans to restore the structure to its 1941 appearance.

Above: Tourists and travelers have been stopping at the historic Eisler Brothers store in Riverton since 1925, when Leo and Lora Williams opened the Williams Store. It became the Eisler Brothers store in 1973. Scott Nelson, president of the Route 66 Association of Kansas, runs the Eisler Brothers Old Riverton Store today.

Right: At Seventh and Main Streets in Galena, a mural celebrating Route 66 was dedicated during festivities surrounding the 2013 Route 66 International Festival in Joplin. Designed by Chris Auckerman and Jon White of Images in Tile, it is composed of 416 fifteen-inch (thirty-eight-centimeter) tiles.

During the 1930s and 1940s, the population of Galena plummeted and many of the elaborate buildings on Main Street vanished. Baxter Springs fared a little better as it was the financial capital of the mining district and the economy was more diversified. The town never allowed mining within the city limits and many mining executives lived there.

Interstate 44 opened in 1961 and bypassed Kansas completely in order to connect to the Will Rogers Turnpike in Oklahoma, which had opened in 1957.

In 1961, a bypass was completed around the Rainbow Curve and the Brush Creek Bridge north of Baxter Springs. In 1963, Route 66 was relocated in Galena from Main Street to Seventh Street, angling northward near Mineral Avenue to become a four-lane divided highway and connect with Missouri's new 66 just east of the state line.

The Kansas Historic Route 66 Association was founded in 1990 and led preservation efforts that saved the Brush Creek Bridge. The Route 66 Association of Kansas is another group formed to preserve the Route 66 heritage. In Galena, the "Four Women on the Route" started a revival by fixing up an old gas station and rescuing the old tow truck that inspired a beloved character from the movie *Cars*.

A journey along Route 66 in Kansas still appeals to those who think that the journey is just as important as the destination. It reconnects us with a sense of community, with an America that's not all franchised, sanitized, wired in, and in a hurry. That's not bad for thirteen miles of roadway.

Above: The old road continues past the bridge and enters Baxter Springs as Fiftieth Street, which turns into Willow Street to join US 69A Highway south, the old Military Road. Just past Ninth Street, a restored 1930s-era Phillips 66 Station houses a Route 66 Visitors Center, staffed by knowledgeable and helpful locals. Although the Baxter Drug Store across the street from the Route 66 Visitors Center in Baxter Springs is now a Walgreens, the vintage sign remains.

Top left: Continuing west through the roundabout at US Highway 400 on Beasley Road, it's a short distance to the precious Brush Creek or Rainbow Bridge. It's the last Rainbow marsh arch–type bridge on Route 66, although they were once common. It was nearly demolished like two others on 66, but the Kansas Route 66 Association mobilized to save it and it can still be driven across today.

Bottom left: Baxter Springs was known as "The First Cowtown in Kansas" a tough, violent, and raucous place where longhorns were driven from Texas. Mining and trucking later became the main industries. The Café on the Route is located in the former Crowell Bank Building, said to have been robbed by some members of the James Gang, without their leader, in 1876.

ROADSIDE
ATTRACTION

THE ROUTE, BAXTER SPRINGS, KANSAS

The café was formerly the Crowell Bank, which Jesse James
1876. It is currently a restaurant and bed and breakfast.

Chapter 4

Sooner or Later We'll Get There

Oklahoma is the heart of Route 66. More miles of Route 66 remain in Oklahoma than in any other state. This is where John Steinbeck called 66 "The Mother Road," and the Dust Bowl gave us some of its most enduring images. The highway was also named for Oklahoma's wisecracking cowboy and homespun philosopher, Will Rogers. And the very idea of Route 66 was hatched in the mind of Cyrus Avery of Tulsa. Oklahoma is also the birthplace of Phillips 66 gasoline and was the home of Andy Payne, winner of one of the most amazing athletic events of all time: the 1928 transcontinental footrace that helped put 66 on the map.

Much of Oklahoma was untamed when it joined the Union in 1907. There were more miles of rail line in the young state than decent roads. Here too, the private promoters were laying out their routes with

Right: Banners proclaim that Route 66 through Commerce is known as Mickey Mantle Boulevard after the hometown hero and New York Yankees legend. His boyhood home is located at 319 South Quincy. A monument at Mickey Mantle Field also honors "The Mick."

Opposite: Rooms sign points the way to privacy at this one-time Oklahoma brothel along Route 66. *Brad Remy/Shutterstock*

glamorous names such as the Albert Pike Highway, the Jefferson Highway, the Kansas City–Tulsa Short Line and the King of Trails. W. H. "Coin" Harvey was one of those promoters who saw that a highway would boost his business.

Harvey owned the luxurious Monte Ne Resort near Rogers, Arkansas, and formed the Ozark Trails Association in 1913 to promote a network of roads that would bring vacationers to his front door. The main route was between St. Louis and Romeroville, New Mexico, passing through Oklahoma. The OTA erected tall obelisks at key intersections along the route, including one in downtown Miami and the obelisk that still stands outside of Stroud. Each one of the obelisks also gave the distance to Monte Ne. Cyrus Avery, at that time a Tulsa county commissioner, was also the vice president of the OTA.

Harvey was concerned only with promoting his resort. But Avery also owned a business, the Olde English Inn and Service Station on the eastern outskirts of Tulsa. He made sure the Ozark Trails Route came past his establishment. By this time, the states and the federal government were taking action to eliminate the confusing system of named highways. Avery was named to the fledgling Oklahoma Highway Commission in 1923. Perhaps more importantly, he became a leader in the American Association of State Highway Officials (AASHTO) and found himself a member of the board that would recommend routes for the proposed federal system.

Avery proposed a national highway slashing southwest from Chicago through his hometown of Tulsa and then on to Los Angeles. The proposal flew in the face of the other highways proposed by the board, all of which were true east-west or north-south routes. But Avery ensured that the proposed highway from Chicago to Los Angeles would roughly follow the Ozark Trails Route and the Kansas City, Fort Scott & Tulsa Short Line. West of Oklahoma City, it would mostly follow the old Postal Highway from Fort Smith, Arkansas, to Amarillo, Texas. In 1924, those routes had been designated as Oklahoma State Routes 7 and 3, respectively.

When Route 66 was commissioned, less than one-fourth of the roadway in Oklahoma was paved, and the pavement between Miami and Afton was just one lane wide. The route zigzagged along the township and section lines in eastern Oklahoma. At Bridgeport, it made a sudden

Above: A Route 66 shield is painted on the "Sidewalk Highway." This stretch of 15.4 miles (25 kilometers) of nine-foot-wide pavement was constructed in 1922 between Miami and Afton. This section became part of Route 66 in 1926 and was bypassed in 1937. Local traffic is destroying these precious and fragile fragments.

Opposite: Miami, pronounced "My-AM-uh," was the first town chartered in the Indian Territory. It was originally known as Jimtown because four residents shared that name. This landmark sign featuring a cuckoo is the last of its kind. The Ku-Ku chain of hamburger restaurants had more than two hundred locations during the 1960s, with buildings designed as giant cuckoo clocks. A bird at the top of the building chimed every hour. Eugene Waylan kept this location going after the chain folded and kept the 1965 vintage sign.

Top: The Buffalo Ranch was a classic roadside attraction complete with forty wild bison, other livestock, and American Indian dances. Russell and Allene Kay opened the tourist spot at US Highway 66 and US Highway 59 in July 1953. Betty Wheatley ran the adjacent Dairy Ranch for forty-two years. The Buffalo Ranch was demolished in 1998, and just a few buffalo remain behind the modern convenience store that took its place.

Above: Afton was founded in 1886 and named for Afton Aires, the daughter of a Scottish railroad surveyor. The surveyor named his daughter after the Afton River in his native Scotland. The ruins of the old Avon Court remain a symbol of the days when Afton bustled with Route 66 traffic. *Judy Hinckley*

Above right: In Afton, vintage signage marks the former Eagle D-X station that became the Afton Station Visitors Center, once operated by the late Laurel Kane. The station opened in 1933, and Laurel and David, her husband at the time, began restoration in 2000. Afton Station still features a collection of rare vintage Packard automobiles.

loop to cross a rickety toll bridge over the Canadian River. An important politician, who charged steep tolls, owned the bridge. A 1934 realignment turned Bridgeport into a virtual ghost town.

The images of choking black dust clouds and overloaded jalopies are enduring symbols of Route 66 during the 1930s. Drought, dust, and economic depression drove up to four hundred thousand Oklahoma residents to seek a new life in the West. Derided as "Okies," they found low wages and deplorable living conditions.

But Steinbeck's "Road of Flight" also provided an economic lifeline for those who stayed to operate cafés, motels, and gas stations. Government relief programs also put men to work improving the highway. Route 66 was fully paved to two lanes across the state as of September 13, 1937, when Governor E. W. Marland dedicated fourteen miles (twenty-three kilometers) of new pavement replacing the "Sidewalk Highway."

During World War II, leisure travel slowed and the US 66 Highway Association faded away. But Route 66 became a vital route for the military, linking installations such as the Clinton Naval Air Station, Tinker Field in Oklahoma City, and the Douglas bomber factory in Tulsa. Another great migration took place, as many headed west to seek work in the defense plants.

Roadside attractions using Western and American Indian imagery sprang up quickly after the war. There were also notorious "tourist traps" such as some of the snake pits in western Oklahoma, which lured tourists into rigged games of chance.

In 1947, the US Highway 66 Association was reorganized, operated by Jack and Gladys Cutberth out of their home in Clinton, Oklahoma. They were able to boast "800 miles [1,300 kilometers] of 4-lane highway," because a major transformation was taking place. The modern highway brought safety and convenience, but had dire consequences for those depending on Route 66 traffic.

In 1947, Governor Roy J. Turner proposed toll roads to replace Route 66 between Oklahoma City and Tulsa. Despite opposition from communities along the route, the Turner Turnpike between Oklahoma City and Tulsa opened in 1953. The Will Rogers Turnpike opened from Tulsa to the Missouri line in 1957, and both became part of Interstate 44.

During the 1950s, Governor Raymond Gary pushed to bring the current Route 66 in western Oklahoma up to interstate standards with

Top: Route 66 through Foyil is signed as Andy Payne Boulevard in honor of the nineteen-year-old part Cherokee youth from Foyil who won the 1928 Bunion Derby. The derby was a transcontinental footrace that made Route 66 famous.

Above: The Chelsea Motel served weary travelers from 1936 to 1976. The sign dates to 1946 and was erected by the owners at that time, Ted and Mildred Noland. Follow Route 28A a few miles to the east to see the world's largest totem pole at folk artist Ed Galloway's Totem Pole Park.

Left: Vinita was named in honor of sculptress Vinnie Ream, who created statues of Abraham Lincoln and Sequoyah for the US Capitol building. Vinita is home to Clanton's Café. The café, marked by a simple "EAT" sign, was opened by "Sweet Tater" Clanton in 1927 and was rebuilt after a fire in December 1997.

A friendly blue whale suddenly appears along Route 66 at Catoosa. Hugh Davis, former director of Tulsa's Mohawk Park Zoo, built it for his wife Zelta. They ran a swimming hole and roadside zoo here from 1970 to 1988. The Blue Whale was restored in 1997.

four-lane business routes through the communities. The interstate was completed through Oklahoma City in 1967. Yukon and El Reno were bypassed in 1969 and I-40 around Weatherford, Clinton, Canute, Elk City, and Sayre opened in 1970. The final segment, bypassing Erick and Texola, opened in 1975.

Route 66 was officially decommissioned in 1985. Sometimes, it is relegated to a mere frontage road or is cut off by the interstate in Oklahoma. But in the communities, Route 66 is still the main street or an alternative to those who shun the turnpikes. It is still a vital road and a major tourist destination. The "kicks" are waiting at the next I-40 off-ramp.

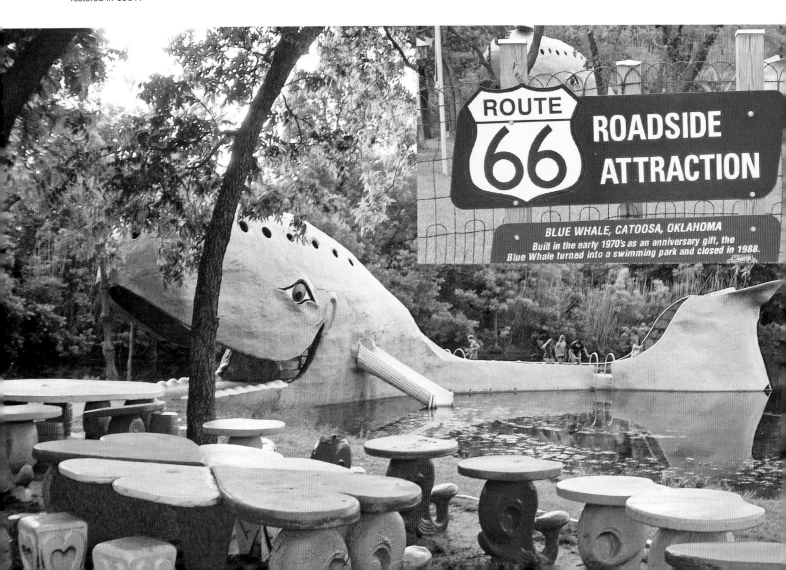

ROUTE **66** ROADSIDE ATTRACTION

BLUE WHALE, CATOOSA, OKLAHOMA
Built in the early 1970's as an anniversary gift, the Blue Whale turned into a swimming park and closed in 1988.

Left: At Claremore, the Will Rogers Memorial and Museum honors the hometown hero who never met a man he didn't like. The comic and homespun philosopher rests in a tomb overlooking the Tiawah Valley. The memorial reads: "If you live life right, death is a joke as far as fear is concerned." Behind the tomb is a statue of Rogers atop his favorite horse, Soapsuds.

In addition to Will Rogers, Claremore is also the hometown of singer Patti Page and playwright Rollie Lynn Riggs. He wrote *Green Grow the Lilacs*, the basis for the musical *Oklahoma*. Claremore was once famous as "Radium Town," with bathhouses offering a soak in the foul-smelling mineral water touted as having healing qualities.

Above: Red and Sally Oats owned the Round-Up Motel in Claremore. The sign for the motel featured a cowboy blowing animated neon smoke rings with his cigar. But the sign came down and the motel was demolished in 2001.

Above: The Will Rogers Motor Court in Tulsa opened in 1941, and owners Paul and Dora Johnson added the classic sign with the rearing horse and rider in 1951. The Will Rogers Motor Court and the sign are both lost landmarks.

Above: The Cyrus Avery Centennial Plaza, at Southwest Boulevard and Riverside Drive at the Eleventh Street Bridge honors the Father of Route 66 with plaza, skywalk, and a bronze sculpture entitled "East Meets West." Future plans include a visitor center and museum. The concrete art-deco Eleventh Street Bridge was completed in 1917 and closed years ago, but it has been renamed in honor of Avery.

Route 66 crosses the Arkansas River and heads into Red Fork on Southwest Boulevard. The first oil well in Tulsa County was completed in Red Fork on June 25, 1901. Red Fork was annexed into the City of Tulsa in October 1927. There is also a former Route 66 bypass route in Tulsa, established along Skelly Drive in 1951. After improvements were completed in 1959, Skelly was designated as Interstate 44 and US 66. Past Red Fork, Route 66 originally followed Southwest Boulevard and Sapulpa Road. The route was shifted to today's State Highway 66 in 1951.

Above right: The Rock Café in Stroud dates back to 1939. Current owner Dawn Welch made it one of the route's most popular stops. In fact, the character Sally Carrera in the movie *Cars* was inspired by Dawn.

Left: Isaac Burnaman constructed his El Reposo Tourist Camp of concrete and stucco in 1933 and it later became the 66 Motel. The motel was torn down on June 26, 2001.

Opposite top: Beatrice Foods erected this big neon sign advertising Meadow Gold milk in 1934 atop a building at Eleventh Street and Lewis. The building closed in 2004, but the sign was restored with help from the Tulsa Foundation for Architecture and the National Park Service. In 2009, it was placed atop a pavilion.

Opposite far left: The neon cactus still flickers at the Desert Hills Motel, opened in 1957 on a small lot on East Eleventh Street in Tulsa. The units were built at angles in order to make the best use of the small space. The motel is fading, but the sign makes a great photo op.

Opposite left: Tally's Good Food Café looks like it could have been around since the heyday of Route 66. It's been a Tulsa landmark since 1987. Tally's is probably best known for its massive cinnamon rolls, and the menu has retro flavor. *Judy Hinckley*

Rest Stop

Phillips 66

Route 66 has always been about turning a buck, selling something to someone. For one company, a last-minute decision to cast its fate with Route 66 still pays off today. The Phillips Petroleum Company took the familiar double sixes and a design based on the federal highway shields just as Route 66 was capturing the imagination of the public, and the firm never regretted it. Here's the story of how Route 66 and the Phillips Petroleum Company became synonymous.

In 1903, the lavish but temporary palaces of the Louisiana Purchase Exposition in St. Louis were still under construction but were already attracting crowds. While on a business trip from his home in Creston, Iowa, banker and

Frank and L. E. Phillips

entrepreneur Frank Phillips decided to stop and see how the Iowa building on the fairgrounds was coming along. He ran into an acquaintance from back home, a preacher just back from the Indian Territory, an area just to the east of the Oklahoma Territory at the time. The preacher regaled Frank Phillips with stories of the oil rising from the ground like water, of the cowboys and Indians and fortunes being made and lost in one day. When the Reverend Larrabee finished his stories, Frank Phillips knew where he would make his mark.

Frank Phillips came to the oil boomtown of Bartlesville, Indian Territory, and saw the reverend was right, and he remembered all the cars he had seen in St. Louis. With money from his father-in-law and with his brother Lee as partner, he acquired leases, hired a driller, and got to work. His fledgling Anchor Oil and Gas Company had some success with its first well in June 1905, but the well soon fizzled. The next two wells were dry. But on the fourth try, the Phillips brothers hit it big with a well on Delaware tribal land he had leased that actually was allotted to an eight-year-old Delaware named Anna Anderson. The Anna Anderson Number 1 sent

oil gushing into the Oklahoma sky on September 6, 1905.

After the well came in, Frank and L. E. Phillips also went into banking. The new bank loaned money to a shady-looking character named Henry Starr without knowing he was the nephew of the "Bandit Queen," Belle Starr, and a man who once robbed two banks in an hour. But Starr paid back the loan and somehow, on a frontier where bank robberies were as common as oil wells, none of the banks operated by the Phillips brothers were ever robbed.

On November 16, 1907, the Oklahoma and Indian territories were combined to become the forty-sixth state in the Union. Fortunes were being made and lost in a single day, and Tulsa, once a little settlement known as "Tulsey Town," was emerging as the headquarters of the oil barons. Meanwhile, a man who started out tinkering in his garage in Detroit was about to change the oil industry and American society forever. Henry Ford was going to put America on wheels.

Prior to the invention of the internal combustion engine, gasoline was considered a useless byproduct of the distillation of crude to produce kerosene. Cars had been powered by steam and electricity as well as gasoline, but the internal combustion engine proved to be the most efficient. But as the Phillips brothers were striking it big, the automobile was still a plaything for the rich. That changed in 1908 when the Ford Motor Company introduced the Model T, the first car for the masses. In

1909, 828,000 horse-drawn vehicles were in the United States and 125,000 automobiles. By 1929, more than two million motor vehicles were being produced annually and an auto trade journal reported four thousand horse-drawn vehicles remained.

But Frank and L. E. Phillips had decided they wanted out of the oil business in order to concentrate on banking and had even begun to sell off their petroleum assets when a single pistol shot thousands of miles away plunged the world into war. The Phillips brothers knew the machinery of modern warfare would need their black gold. Fortunately, they had held onto their leases on Osage land and struck a massive gusher there on March 21, 1917. Frank Philips was destined to stay in the oil industry. On June 13, 1917, they consolidated their assets and went public. The Phillips Petroleum Company was born just as the demand from overseas soared. The company also became a major supplier of natural gas.

Frank Phillips also foresaw that the aviation industry would create demand for his products at the same time that he was looking for a way to get more recognition for his brand. Phillips Petroleum earned huge headlines when it sponsored the winner in the 1927 Dole Derby. Pineapple magnate James Dole had put up $25,000 for the first commercial pilot to make it from San Francisco to Hawaii. Pilot Arthur Goebel and navigator William Davis made the flight aboard the *Woolaroc,* named after Frank Phillips's lodge back in Oklahoma.

Six men and one woman, aviatrix Mildred Doran, died trying. But Phillips Petroleum had conquered the skies and was about to conquer the highways.

Phillips Petroleum researchers in Burbank, California, dubbed the "Whiz Kids," came up with a higher-gravity mix of naphtha and natural gasoline. The mixture boasting "controlled volatility" made it easier for vehicles to start in the winter and provided faster acceleration. The gravity rating could be changed from month to month to match the weather. The new fuel had an adjustable gravity range of sixty-six, extremely high at a time when higher gravity rather than higher octane was considered the mark of quality.

Now the new gas needed a name and Frank Phillips headed up a committee charged with finding one. There was talk of the current trend of combining a name with a number, as exemplified by Heinz 57, and it was noticed almost immediately that the original gravity rating of the fuel was 66. But, since the company planned to adjust the rating between 60.6 and 70.4 to match the weather, the idea of being wedded to a single number was discarded. Time was running out when Frank Phillips called the executives together.

One of those executives was John Kane, who headed for Bartlesville in a company car being used to test the new fuel and driven by Salty Saltwell. They were traveling at a good clip along one of the federal highways commissioned only a year earlier when Kane exclaimed, "This car goes like sixty on

Phillips 66 neon on display in the museum at Times Beach, Missouri

our new gas." Salty shot back, "Sixty nothing! We're going sixty-six." They realized they were doing sixty-six on Route 66, the highway that just happened to run through the heart of the projected marketing territory for the new gasoline. They shared the observation at the meeting the following day.

Classic batwing design on Route 66 Albuquerque, New Mexico

Phillips 66 cottage-style design at Red Oak II near Carthage, Missouri

Frank Phillips later wrote that the phrase "Phillips 66" sounded catchy, even though it really didn't describe the product at all. But they were up against the deadline and they made what he called a "hasty decision" to use Phillips 66. Frank wrote that they never regretted it. In November 1927, the company opened its first refinery, a small facility outside the oil boomtown of Borger, Texas.

There were plenty of legends about how the name was born. One enduring but false story was that Frank and L. E. Phillips had only $66 to their name when the first well came in. Another theory was that a Phillips official had won that first refinery in Borger during a craps game, when the owner had the misfortune of rolling the bones and coming up with double sixes. Yet another myth claims the name was chosen because there are sixty-six books in the Bible.

By the time the new gasoline came out, the roadside was already lined with gas stations, and the competition was fierce. Frank Phillips told his sales staff

to pick the most saturated market in the Midwest and go at the competition, reasoning that the gas would be a success if it could sell in a tough market. Marketing manager Oscar Cordell chose Wichita, Kansas, and the first Phillips 66 station opened at 805 East Central Avenue on November 19, 1927. Newspaper ads ran featuring an illustration of the *Wooloroc*, and Virginia Wilson of Wichita posed as an aviatrix with the slogan "Phill-up to Fly," made a big splash. The station sold out of the first shipment of fuel within twenty-four hours.

Phillips Petroleum used a standardized Cotswald cottage design for its early stations, designed to blend in with the neighborhoods and make the consumer feel comfortable. Similar to a design used by the Pure Oil Company, they were initially painted white with black trim. But within a year, the color scheme was changed to dark green with orange and blue trim that made them instantly recognizable to the motorist. Each featured a tapering false chimney with a backlit "P" affixed to it. There was no "66" at first, only the round logo. The familiar six-pointed black- and-orange design based on the highway shields came around in 1930.

Restored, original-style Phillips 66 stations can be found all along Route 66, including the first one constructed in Texas at McLean. Others can be found in Chandler and Tulsa, Oklahoma, as well as Baxter Springs, Kansas, in Cuba, Missouri, and at Red Oak II near Carthage, Missouri. The cottage-

designed stations were often later repurposed, including several in the St. Louis area that became used car lots. One of the iconic red-and-black shields hangs today at the Smithsonian Institution in Washington, DC.

Phillips contributed to one of the great fads of the Route 66 era. In 1951, the firm entered the plastics business and one of the products it developed was a polyolefin plastic called Marlex. The Wham-O Manufacturing Company used Marlex to produce that beloved toy that swept the nation during the 1950s—the hula hoop.

The company changed to a red-and-white logo in 1959 and also redesigned its stations for the interstate age. The firm employed an exaggerated modern design by Clarence Reinhardt it called Harlequin, featuring an extended canopy sometimes labeled as a batwing. Reinhardt was said to have been inspired by the drive-ins of Los Angeles. These former stations are still relatively common today, many now housing other auto-related businesses. Notable examples still in existence include the former Herbert Martin station on Sixth Street in Amarillo, Texas; one serving as a used car lot on Central Avenue in Albuquerque, New Mexico; and a couple in the St. Louis area.

Of course today, Phillips 66 stations have a modern design that doesn't really stand apart from the countless other convenience store and self-service filling stations. But one thing has not changed. The company logo is still based on the Route 66 shield.

Above: Stroud was a wild place during the Indian Territory days but is a quiet, small town today. Just a few blocks from the Rock Café, the Skyliner Motel on Main Street opened in 1950 and retains its classic neon sign.

Left: Trader James W. Stroud founded Stroud in 1892, as a trading post six miles (ten kilometers) from the Sac and Fox Indian Reservation. Stroud had no shortage of saloons or wild cowboys, due to its proximity to the dry Indian Territory. Things settled down in 1907 when statehood arrived and brought prohibition with it.

Above: Pop's is a relative newcomer to the route, opening in 2007. The giant soda bottle lights up at night and tells one all they need to know about what's inside: hundreds of different brands of soda.

Above right: In 1954 Route 66 between Edmond and Oklahoma City moved to the Northeast Expressway, now Interstate 44, and the Clock Inn opened on the new highway. The motel is gone, but its huge sign with a swinging pendulum stands at the Muscle Car Ranch in Chickasha.

Right: There's only a small sign, but the Round Barn is Arcadia's best-known landmark. William H. Odor built it in 1898. Though challenging to construct, such barns better withstood windstorms. Restoration was completed in 1992. Today it is a Route 66 roadside attraction and venue for dances and other activities.

Opposite: Wellston had the dubious honor of being the first community bypassed by a new roadway designated as State Highway 66. The notorious Wellston Gap wasn't paved until 1933, because the state had promised Route 66 would pass through town, and the US government demanded a bypass. The state was forced to pave the route through town at its own expense, creating the first State Highway 66. The Wellston Route became State Highway 66B when Route 66 was decertified in 1985. The bypass became State Highway 66.

Right: A giant sheet-metal milk bottle tops the former Milk Bottle Grocery on Classen Boulevard in Oklahoma City. The building's odd shape is because the streetcar line met Classen at an angle. Over the years, the milk bottle has advertised Steffen's Dairy, Townley's Dairy, and today Braum's.

Far right: The 66 Bowl opened in March 1959 and closed in August 2010. The sign was auctioned off and the landmark was converted to an Indian grocery store.

Below right: The route follows State Highway 66 through Warr Acres and Bethany. The older route skirts the northern shore of Lake Overholser, where it is necessary to double back to see the 1924 Overholser Bridge. Perhaps a stop at the Route 66–themed park is in order before heading back west to State Highway 66 and Yukon, where the skyline is dominated by the Yukon's Best Flour mill. Yukon is the hometown of country music legend Garth Brooks.

Opposite: The 1930s-era concrete continues straight toward Hydro, rising and falling through the creek valleys. Past the Hydro junction, watch for the lonely combination gas station and residence where Lucille Hammons, the "Mother of the Mother Road," welcomed travelers until she died in 2002. Lucille's Roadhouse in Weatherford is a tribute to her.

Opposite top far right: El Reno was named after nearby Fort Reno, which was established in 1874 and housed some of the famous Buffalo Soldiers black cavalry units. German POWs were housed there during World War II. Today the fort is open to visitors and is home to an agricultural research center. El Reno is also headquarters for the Cheyenne-Arapaho Tribe. The Big 8 Motel and Room 117 were featured in the 1988 film *Rain Man*. The sign was altered to read "Amarillo's Finest" for the movie. A private collector purchased the sign in 1999, and the motel was demolished in 2005.

Opposite far right: In 1939, Chester and Gladys Glancy chose the site for their new motel in Clinton because it was next to the busy Pop Hicks Restaurant. The sign that stands today was added when the Glancy was enlarged and remodeled in 1948. New owners Jay and Sam Patel renovated the Glancy in 2010.

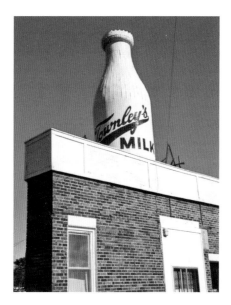

Right: The Oklahoma Route 66 Museum in Clinton is the best of the museums dedicated to the Mother Road. Originally the Western Trails Museum, the renamed museum devoted to Route 66 opened on September 23, 1995. The Oklahoma Historical Society operates it. Jack and Gladys Cutberth ran the National US Highway 66 Association from their Clinton home for twenty-eight years.

The original Route 66 followed Frisco and Tenth through the heart of Clinton, curving south of town under and then alongside Interstate 40. The route crosses to the north side through Foss and crosses a couple more times before rolling into Canute.

Bottom right: Former cotton farmers Woodrow and Viola Peck opened the Cotton Boll Motel in Canute in 1960. Businesses fell off after Interstate 40 opened in 1970 and they sold the sixteen-unit motel in 1979. The motel is now a private residence, but the sign still stands.

Far left: The West Winds Motel in Erick ceased operation years ago and is now a private residence. The fading sign with its bucking bronco remains. The West Winds was constructed shortly after World War II, and Floyd Pamplin operated it for many years.

Left: Elk City hosts the National Route 66 Museum where visitors find a fourteen-foot-tall Kachina named "Myrtle." Myrtle once stood in front of Reese and Wanda Queenan's Trading Post west of town. Queenan served as museum curator and inspired the character of Lizzie in the movie *Cars.*

Below: Travelers came from all over the world to Erick to meet Harley and Annabelle Russell, who called themselves the Medicore Music Makers and offered impromptu performances at their Sandhills Curiosity Shop. The shop was crammed with vintage signs, none of which were for sale. The Route 66 community lost Annabelle in 2014.

Chapter 5

Cowboys and Cadillacs

At first, private trails also ran across the Texas Panhandle. The route that became US 66 was known as the Postal Highway east of Amarillo and the Ozark Trails Route west of Amarillo. The Ozark Trails route came into Amarillo from Wellington and then headed west, connecting with the National Old Trails Road at Las Vegas, New Mexico. The 1919 book *Ozark Trails Route* made no special mention of Amarillo. Vega and Glenrio were the only Texas communities highlighted as "live towns that are taking a public spirited interest in promoting this route." In other words, they paid.

When the federal highway system was approved in 1926, not a single mile of concrete had been poured in Texas and motorists had to open gates between Shamrock and Amarillo. The first hard-surfaced section was in the San Jacinto Heights area of Amarillo, paved with brick in 1927.

Since the major cities of Texas were far to the south, there was little interest in improving Route 66. A dirt section between Alanreed and Groom became infamous as the Jericho Gap, where thick mud trapped vehicles.

The runners in the Bunion Derby endured snow, sleet, and mud in their six-day journey across the Golden Spread. Ninety-three runners remained when they left Glenrio on April 4, 1928. In addition to the weather, the mud of the dreaded Jericho Gap caused several injuries.

Above: In June 1952 a marker was erected at the state line near Shamrock dedicating Route 66 as the Will Rogers Highway. That marker disappeared over the years, but a new granite marker was dedicated in 2008.

Opposite: The Paramount Theater in Amarillo, Texas, dates to 1932. *Brian S./Shutterstock*

Top: "Here's where the snakes are" blared the homemade signs at E. Mike Allred's snake pit on Route 66 at Alanreed. E. Mike was a gruff former carnival man who was also known for breeding "Supernatural Raccoons" with glowing eyes. *Devil's Rope Museum*

Above right: Shamrock is the first town encountered by the westbound Route 66 traveler in Texas and was named by an Irish immigrant. The town's most famous landmark is the Tower Station and U-Drop Inn Café, constructed by John Tindall and R. C. Lewis. It opened on April 1, 1936, and a local youth won $50 for suggesting the name U-Drop Inn for the café. The U-Drop Inn closed in 1995, but the building is now a visitor center. The amazing neon was the inspiration for Ramone's House of Body Art in fictional Radiator Springs, the setting for the film *Cars.*

Above: "A tribute to barbed wire" welcomes visitors to the Devil's Rope and Old Route 66 Museum at McLean. Inside are barbed-wire sculptures, tools, and displays of military "war wire." The Route 66 portion was the first museum dedicated to the fabled highway.

This section of Texas was hit hard by the same drought that drove so many farmers out of Oklahoma. The Panhandle endured 192 "dusters" between 1933 and 1936. About 35 percent of the farmers in the region left between 1935 and 1937.

But Route 66 provided an economic lifeline for those who remained behind, and government relief programs put men to work paving the Jericho Gap. The paving across the state was finally complete in 1937.

In August 1938, Amarillo hosted ceremonies dedicating Route 66 as the Will Rogers Highway. A big parade included Mrs. Will Rogers and Will's favorite horse, Soapsuds. Motorcades from Chicago and Los Angeles met in Amarillo and a pageant with a cast of 1,500 depicted four hundred years of Southwest history. During World War II, leisure travel slowed dramatically and the 66 Highway Association disbanded. But another great migration took place, as families headed west to seek jobs at defense plants and facilities such as the Pantex Plant and the Amarillo Army Airfield.

In 1947, the US Highway 66 Association was reorganized and could boast 66 had "800 miles of 4-lane highway." But the section of two-lane between Shamrock and Amarillo became known as "Bloody 66."

By 1947, Route 66 had been improved to four lanes from the Oklahoma line almost to Groom, and from Amarillo to Bushland by 1954.

Inspired by the autobahns of Germany he saw during World War II, President Dwight Eisenhower signed the Interstate Highway Act in 1956, providing federal money for a new system of superhighways. Interstate 40 would replace Route 66 across the panhandle.

Above: The first Phillips 66 station in Texas opened in McLean in 1929, and the Old Route 66 Association of Texas restored the exterior in 1992. Phillips 66 stations used this Tudor cottage design and were painted dark green with orange and blue trim to stand out from competitors.

Above left: The notorious Jericho Gap was an eighteen-mile unpaved stretch of Route 66 between Alanreed and Groom that turned to a sea of mud when it rained. In 1936 a paved highway bypassed it and a four-lane route had been completed by the time this shield was photographed in the 1950s.

Far left: The 66 Courts in Groom opened in 1947 and included a café and gas station. It fell into ruins after Interstate 40 arrived, and a vintage Edsel remained parked out front. It all was demolished in 2005.

Left: "Slim" Windom drove a dump truck during construction of Route 66 in the infamous Jericho Gap. In 1951 he opened the West Wind Motel with his wife, Grace. The West Wind became the Cactus Inn Motel in the 1960s

Above right: Amarillo is Spanish for "yellow," a name inspired by yellow soil. The intersection of US Highway 66 and US Highway 60 formed a triangle on the east side of Amarillo, where former Borger, Texas, Mayor Silas M. Clayton opened the Triangle Motel in 1946. The Triangle closed in 1977.

Above center: Many Route 66 motels in Amarillo used Western imagery to attract business. The original sign in the shape of a cowboy boot remains at the Silver Spur Motel with more modern signage tacked on alongside.

Above left: The Eastridge Bowling Palace in Amarillo, "the most modern and up-to-date in the Southwest," opened in 1959. A more recent addition to the sign notes the name change to Eastridge Lanes.

Opposite: Vintage signs still stand in front of the Cowboy Motel and the Cattleman's Club & Café in Amarillo. The motel was originally named Del Camino, Spanish for "the road." The Cattleman's Club & Café has been in business since 1961.

In 1962 the US Highway 66 Association met in Shamrock and passed a resolution asking highway officials to name the new route from Chicago and Los Angeles as Interstate 66. But the bureaucrats refused. By the 1970s, most of the Mother Road had been replaced by portions of five interstates across the United States: I-55, I-44, I-40, I-15, and I-10.

Route 66 held on a little longer in Texas, because much of Interstate 40 used portions of the route to save construction costs and because of resistance by communities and business owners. It would be 1984 before McLean became the last community in Texas, and the second to last in the nation, to be bypassed. Route 66 was decommissioned in 1985.

But the old road would not die. Travelers from all over the world still seek out the old motels, diners, and tourist traps along the Main Street of America. Route 66 is for those who think that the journey is as important as the destination. There isn't much to see blasting across Texas on Interstate 40 at 75 miles per hour (121 kilometers per hour). The adventure is waiting at the next off-ramp.

The "Great Sign"

Holiday Inn's "Great Sign" is probably the best-known roadside sign in the world, even though the modern corporation shuns it. It inspires mixed emotions on Route 66, as the Holiday Inns arrived at the same time the interstate highway system was replacing Route 66 and the chain motels put many classic Route 66 establishments out of business. But Holiday Inn revolutionized travel, for better or for worse, bringing standardized rates, amenities, and expectations. And they could be found in any big town on Route 66.

The first location opened on August 1, 1952, at 4941 Sumner Avenue on the main route between Memphis and Nashville. Architect Eddie Bluestein coined the name after the 1942 musical *Holiday Inn*, starring Bing Crosby and Fred Astaire.

Franchised locations began opening in 1957, and one thousand locations were nationwide by 1964.

The "Great Sign" became an icon. Each one of the massive signs with the script logo contained 1,500 feet (458 meters) of neon tubing and more than five hundred incandescent bulbs. A large chasing arrow always pointed toward the motel and the tower portion was lit with red, orange, or blue neon.

Memphis artist James Anderson Sr. originally designed the sign. In 1982, the board of directors did away with the sign, and most were sold for scrap.

The first Holiday Inn on Route 66 opened in Springfield, Illinois, in 1959. It was located at the corner of Sixth Street and Linn Street (now Stephenson Drive), and it is now the Route 66 Hotel and Conference Center.

The Joplin, Missouri, Holiday Inn was well known to baseball fans. Harold Young made Mickey Mantle a partner in the Holiday Inn that opened in October 1957 at 2600 Range Line. Mantle was from nearby Commerce, Oklahoma, and had played minor league ball in Joplin. The version of the iconic sign at this Holiday Inn weighed ten thousand pounds and cost $12,500.

The Holiday Inn marquee inspired dozens of signs. In Springfield, Missouri, Rest Haven Motel owner Hillary Brightwell designed one manufactured by Springfield Neon in 1953. But which came first? The Rest Haven sign went up in 1953, just a year after that first Holiday Inn opened. The Rest Haven sign inspired Pete Hudson, owner of the Munger Moss Motel in Lebanon, to create a similar one.

The sign at the King Brothers Motel, outside St. Louis, obviously took its cue from the Holiday Inn.

Travelers embraced standardized motels, but there was a price to be paid. Sitting and chatting in the office or on the front porch of the motel under the buzzing neon sign were replaced by internet bookings. Today, it is possible to check in and out without ever interacting with another human being. In our world of instant gratification and constant movement, even the Holiday Inn sign can inspire nostalgia.

Top: West Sixth Avenue is a vibrant neighborhood of restaurants, nightclubs, and antique stores. It contains dozens of intact structures from the Route 66 era and is listed on the National Register of Historic Places.

Above: West of Amarillo, a row of ten vintage Cadillacs covered with graffiti is half buried in the ground at the same angle as the Pyramid of Cheops. The Cadillac Ranch was created in 1974 by a trio of artists known as the Ant Farm Collective for the eccentric Stanley Marsh 3. In 1997 Marsh decided urban sprawl was encroaching on the Cadillac Ranch. The Caddys were dug up and replanted two miles (three kilometers) to the west. The Amarillo West RV Park pays tribute to the landmark with three Cadillacs displayed at an angle.

Top: In 1962 Bob Lee of the Big Texan Restaurant began offering a free seventy-two-ounce steak dinner, if eaten in one hour. Lee was forced to move to the interstate to stay in business in 1968. He took the sign with him, and the Big Texan is still a favorite with the tourists.

Above: The Golden Light Café on West Sixth Avenue is the oldest restaurant on Route 66 in Texas still operating at the same location. It is named for the western sunrays that light the café in the afternoon.

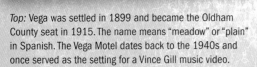

Top: Vega was settled in 1899 and became the Oldham County seat in 1915. The name means "meadow" or "plain" in Spanish. The Vega Motel dates back to the 1940s and once served as the setting for a Vince Gill music video.

Above: Dot Leavitt spent decades gathering signs, antiques, and western artifacts for Dot's Mini-Museum, opened in 1963 in Vega.

Right: The isolated outpost of Landergrin was the home of George and Melba Rook's Route 66 Antiques and the Neon Soda Saloon. George Rook displayed the largest-known collection of Route 66 shields inside. But the store was abandoned and the signs sold off after he died in 1998.

Above: Adrian is proud of its status as the "Geo-mathematical Center of Route 66." A sign in front of the Midpoint Café declares a distance of 1,139 miles (1,834 kilometers) to Chicago and 1,139 miles to Los Angeles and serves as a popular photo stop.

Left: The shattered sign at the Texas Longhorn Motel and Café at Glenrio once declared it was the "Last Stop in Texas" on the east side and "First Stop" in Texas on the west. Glenrio was a busy place that died quickly after Interstate 40 opened in 1973. Only lonely ruins, tumbleweeds, and wandering dogs greet the few visitors today.

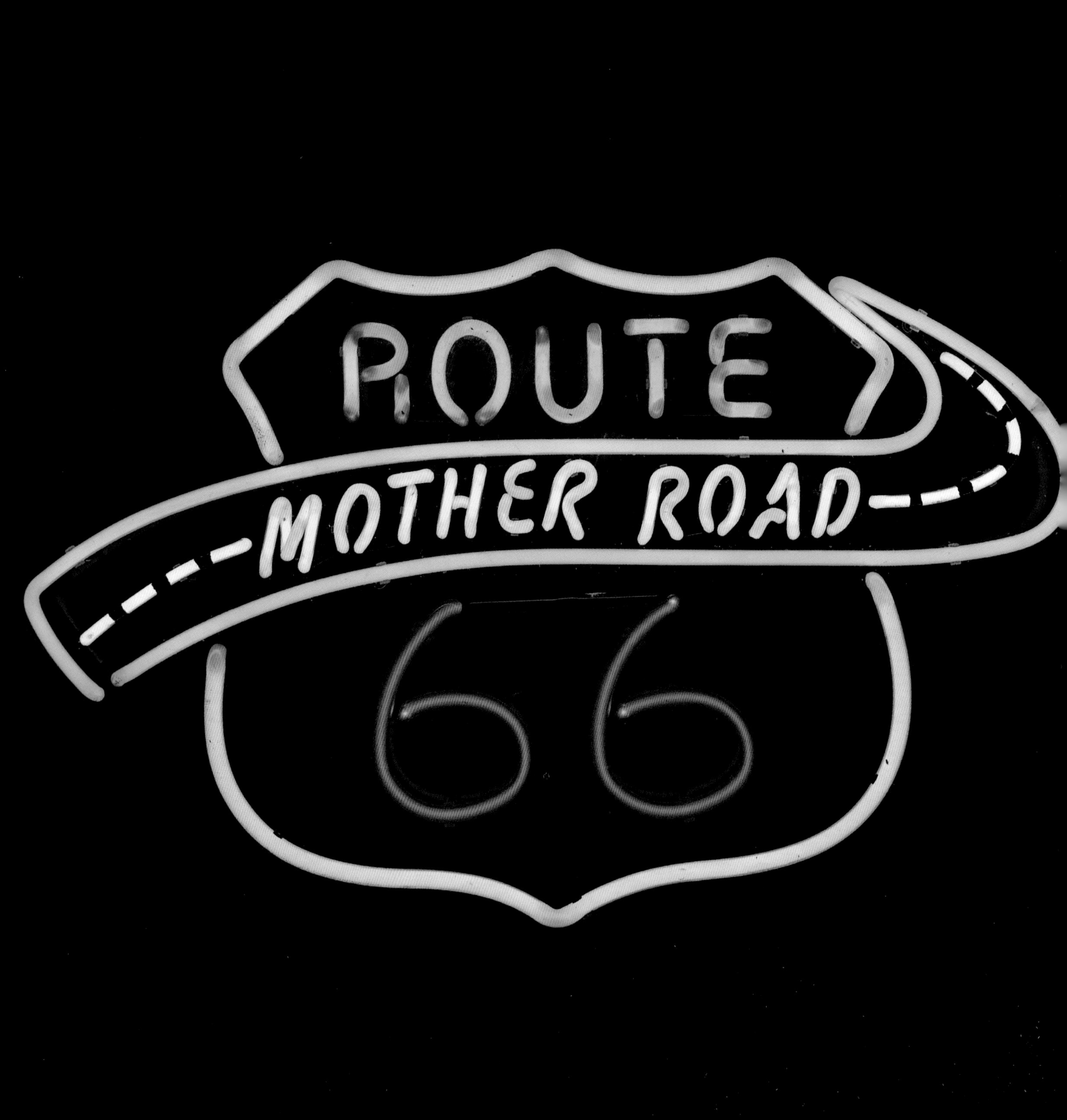
ROUTE
MOTHER ROAD
66

Chapter 6

Enchantment

New Mexico presents an amazing palette of history, scenery, and cultures that all comes together to amaze visitors. Part of Route 66 follows the oldest road in America, the Camino Real de Tierra Adentro, or "Royal Road to the Interior Lands." The route, in use since 1598, linked Mexico City with Santa Fe. Early travelers took the path of least resistance around natural barriers that prevented travel straight east or west and the railroads followed.

The Fred Harvey Company opened the Southwest to mass tourism. After providing Atchison, Topeka & Santa Fe rail travelers with the grandest hotels and dining facilities, Harvey created the Indian Detours. Railroad travelers could take automobile or bus tours for a few days to visit American Indian sites, and then continue their trip by rail. These tours provided some of the impetus for improving the roads, especially the treacherous route over La Bajada Mesa south of Santa Fe. A 1909 automobile race between Albuquerque and Santa Fe took nine and a half hours to cover the sixty miles (ninety-seven kilometers).

East-west travel was accorded little importance when a state highway system was designated in 1914. There was no east-west state route between Santa Rosa and Moriarty.

During the era of the private highway promoters, a pole or fence post might have been emblazoned with multiple symbols for the many routes that often overlapped. Between Tucumcari and Santa Rosa alone, the Panhandle-Pacific Highway, the Atlantic-Pacific Highway, the Texas–New

Above: Old 66 between Glenrio and San Jon is now a lonely road covered with gravel. It crosses old timber bridges and parallels the abandoned railroad right of way. The Endee Grocery and Garage once boasted "Modern Rest Rooms" but is in ruins today. *Judy Hinckley*

Opposite: Neon Route 66 sign in New Mexico. *Brian S./Shutterstock*

Above: Tucumcari is named for the nearby mountain. The name is Comanche and means "lookout." A mural in town recalls the days when billboards for hundreds of miles on Route 66 urged travelers to make it "Tucumcari Tonite."

Opposite: The Teepee Curios sign was one of ten signs restored in 2003 as a joint project of the New Mexico Route 66 Association, the New Mexico Historic Preservation Division, and the National Park Service Route 66 Corridor Preservation Office. *Judy Hinckley*

Mexico Highway, and the Ozark Trails Route all shared the sections of the road that would become Route 66.

C. C. Pyle, the runners, an army of reporters, and the traveling circus accompanying the 1928 Bunion Derby crossed into New Mexico on March 28. The city of Albuquerque banned the racers, because Mayor Clyde Tingley believed Pyle and his people were crooks. The runners were forced to detour another seventeen miles (twenty-seven kilometers) up Tijeras Canyon before a downhill run into Moriarty. Just ninety-three runners were left by the time the dusty caravan made it through Glenrio.

The original Route 66 turned north near today's Exit 273 on Interstate 40, passing through Dilia before joining what is now US Highway 84 to Romeroville. The route then joined US Highway 85 to Santa Fe and along the old Camino Real, entering Albuquerque on Fourth Street. Original Route 66 continued south to Los Lunas before finally turning west. It was a meandering route of 506 miles (815 kilometers), of which only 28 miles (45 kilometers) were paved in 1926. The long Santa Fe loop was necessary to avoid the sandy hills and steep grades west of the Rio Grande, as well as the tire-shredding lava fields near Grants.

The roads were dangerous. The most intimidating was the dizzying plunge down the La Bajada Mesa south of Santa Fe, with its sharp switchbacks and piles of stones serving as guardrails. In April 1930, at a crossing near Isleta, twenty-one people died when a Santa Fe mail train plowed in a Pickwick-Greyhound Bus. Investigators found later that a female passenger was sitting on the bus driver's lap.

A bridge over the Rio Grande at Old Town Albuquerque was constructed in 1931 and completion of the bridge at the Rio Puerco in 1933 finally allowed travelers to head straight west, bypassing Los Lunas. But that route was not designated as Route 66 until a ticked off politician entered the picture.

Arthur T. Hannett, a former mayor of Gallup, lost his bid for reelection as governor in November 1926. Partly in revenge and partly because it just made sense, he ordered construction of a highway between Santa Rosa and Albuquerque. Citizens from towns along other routes vandalized the equipment and the winter weather was brutal. But crews worked double shifts to finish the job before Richard C. Dillon took office on January 1, 1927. Dillon immediately ordered the work halted, but the engineer he sent with the order was delayed by a snowstorm and couldn't find the work crews until January 3. By then, a rough, but usable, road had already been completed.

Route 66 shifted to "Hannett's Joke" in 1937, cutting the mileage across New Mexico from 506 to 399 miles (810 to 642 kilometers). The new highway entered Albuquerque on Central Avenue. In 1935, sixteen tourist camps were along Fourth Street and just three on Central. By 1955, ninety-eight motels were along Central/Route 66.

As speeds and traffic loads increased, the number of accidents grew at an alarming rate. Between 1953 and 1958, one in every five highway fatalities statewide was on Route 66. In August 1958, sixteen people died in just one week on Route 66 in New Mexico.

Because the interstates used a different numbering system, no Interstate 66 would be crossing New Mexico. The first section of Interstate 40 was finished by 1960 between Santa Rosa and a point west of Clines Corners. But it would be some time before the cities were bypassed. State lawmakers passed a measure requiring community approval of a bypass. After the federal government threatened to cut off funds, the measure was repealed in 1966. Communities then worked out deals with the federal government to keep the bypass routes closer to the business districts.

In the late 1960s, there were so many crashes on a forty-mile stretch of Route 66 between Glenrio and Tucumcari that it became known as "Slaughter Lane." Construction of Interstate 40 was held up there due to a dispute over the route around San Jon. The interstate through Albuquerque was finished in 1970. Bypasses were completed at Santa Rosa in 1972, Moriarty in 1973, Grants in 1974, and Gallup in 1980. The section around Tucumcari and San Jon opened in 1981.

Rest Stop

The Blue Swallow

Kevin Muell●

For sailors, a swallow, bluebird, or sparrow symbolized a safe return home. The neon swallows at the most famous motel on Route 66 have symbolized a home away from home for more than seventy-five years. Just as the swallows return to San Juan Capistrano, California, every year, travelers return time and time again to the Blue Swallow Motel. One can sense the spirits of those who have come before and of former owner Lillian Redman. Kevin and Nancy Mueller tirelessly honor and preserve the tradition today.

As the tracks of the Rock Island Railroad pushed west in 1901, a railroad camp named Douglas was established here. It unofficially became known as Six Shooter Siding and was a wild town with every vice found in the west. Within a year, it had been renamed Tucumcari, for the mountain dominating the view.

But the town fathers concocted a more romantic story behind the name. Their legend told of the doomed lovers Tocom and Kari. Kari, the daughter of Apache Chief Wautonomah, decreed that Tocom and another brave, Tonopah,

would duel for the hand of his daughter. Kari hated Tonopah, so when his knife found Tocom's heart, the anguished Kari stabbed Tonopah and plunged the knife into her own heart. The legend says the heartbroken chief named the mountain for Tocom and Kari.

By 1939, Tucumcari businesses were shifting away from the old town center along the railroad to the new corridor along Route 66. Carpenter W. A. Huggins bought the land on March 29, 1939, and began construction of a ten-room motel and a café, which opened by 1940. The original sign featured a swooping blue swallow, but was much smaller than the present sign. Neon artist Joel Rayburn has re-created the original sign, which is now on display at the motel.

Huggins operated the motel for a short time before Rancher Ted Jones and his wife Margie took over. They added a new and bigger office, a small residence, and two more rooms.

Kevin Mueller

Floyd Redman bought the Blue Swallow and gave the motel to his fiancée Lillian as an engagement present in 1958. The current sign was added in 1960.

Lillian Redman came west from Texas with her parents in a covered wagon in 1915 and later worked as a Harvey Girl in Kingman and Winslow, Arizona. She owned and operated a restaurant in Gallup, New Mexico, before returning to Tucumcari in the late 1940s. The Redmans were known for their generosity, sometimes providing free lodging if the guest couldn't afford the price of a room.

Floyd died in 1973 and the arrival of Interstate 40 brought hard times. But Lillian developed a special connection with Route 66 travelers. She is quoted on the National Park Service website as saying, "I end up traveling the highway in my heart with whoever stops here for the night."

When Lillian operated the motel, each guest received her prayer for travelers, a copy of which is still found in each room.

Greetings Traveler:

In ancient times, there was a prayer for "The Stranger Within our Gates." Because this motel is a human institution to serve people, and not solely a money-making organization, we hope that God will grant you peace and rest while you are under our roof.

May this room and motel be your "second" home. May those you love be near you in thoughts and dreams. Even though we may not get to know you, we hope that you will be as comfortable and happy as if you were in your own house.

May the business that brought you this way prosper. May every call you make and every message you receive add to your joy. When you leave, may your journey be safe.

We are all travelers. From "birth till death," we travel between the eternities. May these days be pleasant for you, profitable for society, helpful for those you meet, and a joy to those you know and love best.

Sincerely yours,
Lillian Redman

Lillian took time with every guest, but time was taking a toll on her. The motel had begun to fade and the electrical system needed an overhaul by the time she sold to Dale and Hilda Bakke in 1998. Lillian died on February 21, 1999, at the age of eighty-nine. Dale and Hilda painstakingly restored the Blue Swallow while preserving its history and charm. More restoration work was completed under the ownership of Bill Kinder and Terry Johnson.

Kevin and Nancy Mueller took over the Blue Swallow in July 2011. They continue to honor Lillian's legacy with their hard work and a seemingly endless supply of energy and warmth. In June 2015, Kevin and Nancy Mueller added this two-thirds-size replica of the original Blue Swallow sign that was created by GlassBoy Studios of Oklahoma City.

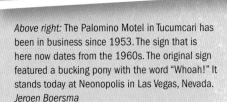

Above right: The Palomino Motel in Tucumcari has been in business since 1953. The sign that is here now dates from the 1960s. The original sign featured a bucking pony with the word "Whoah!" It stands today at Neonopolis in Las Vegas, Nevada. *Jeroen Boersma*

Above left: The Motel Safari is another restored Route 66 gem in Tucumcari. It dates to 1960 and the sign originally had a Best Western logo at the top, replaced with a camel in 1962. Richard Talley renovated the motel in 2008.

Right: Constructed in 1960, the Pony Soldier Motel was located on the eastern end of the motel row in Tucumcari. The sign was updated to showcase modern amenities and still stands. But the motel came down in 2010.

Above: The Lasso Motel in Tucumcari advertised "Color TV by RCA" and remained in business until 2009. After the motel was demolished, the sign stood all alone until being taken down in 2012.

Right: Pearl and Dugan Barnett's Ranch House Café also opened in 1952 and was one of the first in Tucumcari to offer curb service. It was operated along with the Conoco station next door.

Below: The Buckaroo Motel opened in 1952 and originally had a different sign. This one probably dates from around 1963, when the motel changed hands. The Buckaroo is still in business today and the sign comes alive at night.

Bottom: Many memories were made and many Rattler Jumbo burgers with green chile were downed at the Westerner Drive-Inn in Tucumcari from 1949 until 2000. Jack Poer, and later Clinton and Dorothy White, operated it for many years. *Jeroen Boersma*

Right: Jose and Carmen Campos opened La Loma Lodge in 1949, and it remains in the family today. It became the La Loma Motel in the 1950s and this sign probably dates from that era.

Below right: The Sun 'n Sand Motel sign makes use of the sacred sun symbol of the Zia Indians and was restored in 2002. But the motel was fading fast as of 2015. The four points radiate from a circle symbolizing life and the sun. The points represent the four seasons, four directions, parts of the day, and stages of life.

Below: The friendly truck driver on the sign at the Rio Pecos Ranch Truck Terminal at one time waved his neon hand. The City of Santa Rosa was interested in acquiring thc sign in 2003, but the deal fell through, and it continues to fade away.

Bottom left: West of Santa Rosa, the Ozark Trail Route turned north to head for Santa Fe. This marker stood west of Las Vegas, New Mexico. Route 66 followed this route from 1926 until 1937.

Above left: Headed straight west from Santa Rosa along Interstate 40, the highway follows Hannett's Joke, named after the aforementioned governor who bypassed the state capitol when he lost the election. Ahead is one of those tourist stops that still retains much of its old-fashioned feel. Clines Corners offers everything from rubber tomahawks to American Indian art, along with a big selection of Route 66 items.

Above right: South of Santa Fe, the route over La Bajada Mesa (Spanish for "the descent from the mesa") was part of the Camino Real. The road was rebuilt in 1908 by convict and Cochiti Indian labor, and it drops 800 feet (244 m) in 1.6 miles (3 kilometers) with twenty-three hairpin switchbacks. A sign at the top warned: "This road is not foolproof but safe for a sane driver." La Bajada was bypassed in 1932.

South of Santo Domingo, Route 66 passed through eighteen-foot-wide (five-meter) and seventy-five-foot-long (twenty-three-meter) cut through Gravel Hill on the El Camino Real. "The Big Cut" was considered an engineering marvel when it was dug out in 1909. Route 66 was rerouted in 1931, but the cut is still visible from Interstate 25.

Left: The Longhorn Ranch Motel is closed but still stands across from a classic roadside attraction that gave the tourists the Old West they had seen in the movies. The Longhorn Ranch was complete with a saloon, a stagecoach, and a Texas longhorn steer named Babe. Only ruins remain today.

Right: El Comedor de Anayas in Moriarty was in the Anaya family for sixty years and was a favorite with politicians. Jimmy Carter and Bill Clinton were among the visitors. The stunning and rare Roto-Sphere with its neon spikes was added in the 1960s and was restored in 2002.

Don Francisco Cuervo y Valdes, interim governor of New Mexico, established La Villa de San Francisco Xavier de Alburquerque in 1706. The villa was named after the viceroy of New Spain, Don Francisco Fernandez de la Enriquez, and eighth Duke of Alburquerque. (The extra *R* in the city's name disappeared over the years.)

Route 66 originally entered Albuquerque on Fourth Street, where nineteen tourist courts were prior to the 1937 realignment of Route 66 over Central Avenue. Only El Camino Motor Hotel survives today. From 1926 to 1937, Route 66 continued south past the Isleta Pueblo to Los Lunas. Completion of the Rio Puerco Bridge in 1933 allowed traffic to head straight west from Albuquerque and the Laguna Cutoff became part of Route 66 in 1937.

Below: Route 66 plunges down the Tijeras Canyon, going through the Sandia and the Manzano Mountains. The Mountain Lodge offered a splendid setting but was converted to monthly rentals in later years. It burned down on December 18, 2014.

Top left: La puerta is Spanish for "the door," and the La Puerta Lodge features a massive hand-carved door to the old office. It opened in 1949 and still retains the feel of a classic mom-and-pop Route 66–era motel.

Top right: The Pueblo-styled Tewa Lodge at 5715 East Central Avenue opened in 1949. It is still in business and on the National Register of Historic Places. The Tewa neon sign is one of the prettiest on Route 66.

Left: The Pioneer Motel was originally known as the Pioneer Luxury Court and opened in 1949. The current sign and its tall companion were added after an ownership change in 1958.

Above: In 1955 Central Avenue was lined with ninety-eight motels in styles ranging from Southwest motifs to lavish Space Age designs. Many resorted to monthly rentals just to survive after Interstate 40 opened and they became havens for criminals and transients. Many have been demolished, including the Zia Motor Lodge. The star atop the sign once flashed brilliantly.

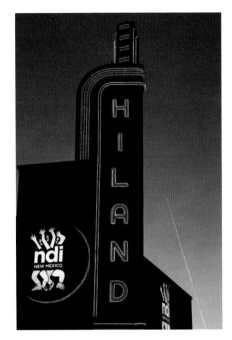

Above: Spectacular signs in Albuquerque aren't just limited to the motels. Garcia's Café has become more famous lately for appearing in the AMC television series *Breaking Bad*, along with many other Albuquerque locations.

Above center: Frank Peloso and family opened the 875-seat Hiland Theater in 1951. In 2009 Bernalillo County leased the shuttered building to the National Dance Institute (NDI) of New Mexico and renovation began. NDI offers performing arts programs for children. *National Dance Institute of New Mexico*

Top right: Kelly's Brew Pub occupies the former Ralph Jones Motor Company Ford dealership and Texaco station, constructed in 1939. Dennis and Janice Bonfantine opened Kelly's here in 2000. *Kelly's Brew Pub*

Center right: Room 114 at the Desert Sands Motel made a bloody appearance in the movie *No Country for Old Men*, and Room 109 is said to be haunted. The words "El Paso" were added to the sign temporarily for the film. An arsonist burned down Desert Sands on May 23, 2016.

Right: The De Anza Motor Lodge was built in 1939 and named for Spanish Lt. Juan Batista de Anza, a former territorial governor portrayed on the sign. The city of Albuquerque purchased the landmark in 2003. In 2015, a developer proposed bringing it back to life as a "condotel."

Above: As of 2016, the City of Albuquerque was hunting for a new place to install the sign from the Aztec Motel. The Aztec opened in 1931, six years before Route 66 came down Central Avenue, and it was the oldest continuously operating motel on Route 66 in New Mexico when it was demolished in 2011.

Far left: The Premiere Motel opened in 1941 and the smaller original sign is still on the property. This 1950s-era sign was restored in 2008, and the renovated motel is now an extended-stay facility.

Left: Nob Hill was Albuquerque's first suburb, and it now has evolved into a cosmopolitan, neon-drenched entertainment district with Route 66-era architecture. The Nob Hill Motel was in business from 1936 to 2006 and was redeveloped for offices and retail in 2009.

Above: Absolutely Neon is just one of the distinctive art galleries and shops in the Nob Hill District. Absolutely Neon restores and maintains much of the historic neon in Albuquerque and showcases the neon artistry of owner Robert Randazzo.

Right: The Route 66 Diner opened in 1987 in the former Sam's Phillips 66 Station, constructed in 1946. Owner Tom Willis quickly rebuilt after a 1995 fire, and the diner offers classic food with a fun retro atmosphere.

Top: A neon dachshund happily munches wieners at the Doghouse on West Central Avenue. The sign probably came from the original location downtown, which opened about 1940. This location, also featured in *Breaking Bad*, opened in the 1960s.

Top left: The Pueblo Deco Kimo Theatre opened in 1927. The name is loosely translated as "King of Its Kind." The city began restoration in 1977, and the theater offers film, musical, and theater performances today.

Center left: The El Don Motel opened in 1946 is still in business today. The sign featuring a cowboy with a flashing neon lariat was restored in 2001.

Bottom left: Just down the street from the El Don, the Monterey Non-Smokers Motel was originally the Davis Court and opened in 1946. It is still highly recommended for Route 66 travelers today.

Above: Built in 1936, the El Vado Motel combined Pueblo and Spanish influences. It was nearly demolished after closing in 2005, but the city took over the property. In 2015, plans were underway to convert part of it to a boutique motel, shops, and a food court.

   The San Felipe de Neri Church dominates the plaza in Old Town, where the Villa de Alburquerque (with that extra *R*) was established in 1706. Because development shifted east to New Albuquerque with the arrival of the railroad, Old Town kept much of its historic charm and today houses 130 shops and restaurants, including La Placita, a restaurant opened in 1931 in a hacienda that dates back to 1706.

Top: West of the Rio Grande, a full arch spans West Central Avenue between Sixty-Fourth and Sixty-Fifth Streets.

Above left: Nine Mile Hill, nine miles (fourteen kilometers) from the center of Albuquerque, offers a view of the city and the Sandia Mountains. This board was one of a series advertising the Rio Puerco Trading Post west of Albuquerque.

Now Route 66 cuts through the heart of the forty-two-square-mile Laguna Pueblo lands. The old highway twists around the beautiful rock formations that the builders of four-lane 66 and Interstate 40 simply blasted through.

Laguna Pueblo was officially established in 1699, named after a nearby lake that no longer exists. The largest of the Keresan-speaking pueblos, it includes the villages of Laguna, Paguate, Encinal, Mesita, Seama, and Paraje. The San Jose de Laguna Church, completed in 1699, dominates the view of Kawaika, or Old Laguna.

Above right: The Grandview Motel was the first motel travelers encountered at the western city limits of Albuquerque. The attractive motel is still in business today, with beautiful multicolored neon on the rooflines.

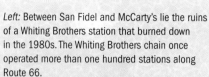

Left: Between San Fidel and McCarty's lie the ruins of a Whiting Brothers station that burned down in the 1980s. The Whiting Brothers chain once operated more than one hundred stations along Route 66.

Bottom left: Three flags stand atop the sign for the Sands Motel in Grants. The motel opened in 1950, and Elvis Presley is reported to have stayed there, although it gets mixed reviews today.

Below: Grants was originally a railroad base camp, established by brothers Angus, Lewis, and John Grant. It was known as Grant's Camp, then Grant's Station, and finally just Grants beginning in 1936. In 1950, rancher Paddy Martinez discovered uranium in the Haystack Mountains west of town, launching a twenty-year-long mining boom. The Uranium Café opened in 1956 and was closed for years, but became Badlands Burgers in 2012.

Above: The Roarin' 20s sign originally stood outside a club in Albuquerque. After the club closed, Eddie McBride brought the sign to his father's Sunshine Café, dance hall, and bar in Gallup. A box reading "The" covers the word "Eddie's" on the sign.

Below right: The area between Grants and Gallup was classic tourist trap country, where the Lost Canyon Trading Post lured tourists with the snake-filled Den of Death. Not to be outdone, the Rattlesnake Trading Post offered a fake giant prehistoric reptile. The businesses at the Continental Divide were once known for prostitution, bar brawls, and fleecing tourists. Things are much calmer there today.

Above right: Many vintage motels remain in Gallup, including the Blue Spruce Lodge. It was once operated by John Milosovich, who became mayor of Gallup when he was just twenty-one.

Above: A classic arch topped with a Route 66 shield stood at the Arizona and New Mexico state line. The westbound side offered best wishes to drivers and asked them to come again to New Mexico. Anyone who made the journey across the Land of Enchantment on Route 66 certainly would want to.

Left: Gallup was established in 1881, named for railroad paymaster David Gallup. Workers would go to Gallup for their pay. The town bills itself as "The Indian Capital" and this giant kachina once stood on Route 66 to welcome travelers.

Right: El Rancho Hotel in Gallup formally opened on December 17, 1937. El Rancho Hotel was built for R. E. Griffith, supposedly the brother of movie magnate D. W. Griffith. It was the headquarters for eighteen movies filmed between 1940 and 1964. Stars who stayed at the "World's Largest Ranch House" include John Wayne, Ronald Reagan, Katherine Hepburn, and Kirk Douglas.

HISTORIC ROUTE 66

MOTEL

QUEEN BEDS WI FI
DIRECTV AND HBO
REFRIGERATOR AND
COFFEE POTS

VACANCY

Approved

Chapter 7

Grand

Natural wonders define Route 66 across Arizona, a link between the Painted Desert, Petrified Forest, Meteor Crater, and the awe-inspiring Grand Canyon. Plenty of human-made diversions are along the way too.

Route 66 is no ordinary road: camels blazed part of it. In 1857 Lt. Edward F. Beale surveyed a wagon road from Fort Defiance, New Mexico Territory, to the Colorado River along the Thirty-Fifth Parallel. The expedition brought along twenty-three camels to test their usefulness in hauling cargo.

The Atlantic & Pacific Railroad (later the Santa Fe) closely followed his camel route, known as Beale's Wagon Road, spawning the communities of Holbrook, Winslow, Flagstaff, Williams, Ash Fork, Seligman, Kingman, and others. The Fred Harvey Company opened Arizona to mass tourism, constructing lavish Harvey Houses that offered Santa Fe Railroad patrons and locals food and accommodations equal to those in the major cities. The Harvey Houses were ready to serve motorists when the automobile age arrived.

In 1909 J. B. Girand was appointed territorial engineer to plot out four roads connecting each of the fourteen Arizona county seats. One of those roads passed through Springerville and St. Johns before picking up the future path of Route 66. Girand's route also dropped south from Kingman through Yucca and Topock to the Colorado River.

Above: The red, yellow, and white signs along Route 66 announce the forthcoming Fort Yellowhorse Trading Post. The state line runs right through the trading post with its fake animals perched on the bluff.

Opposite: Arizona's Historic Route 66 Motel. Pabkov/Shutterstock

Above: More than 200 million years ago, volcanic eruptions felled a stately pine forest when this part of Arizona was a flood plain. Sand and ash covered the trees, and, over the eons, silica replaced the wood. Millions of years later, the sandstone and shale eroded and left the logs on the surface. *Petrified Forest National Park*

Above right: Adam Luna of the Rainbow Rock Shop made these roadside dinosaurs in Holbrook. A sign warned there was a twenty-five-cent charge to photograph them. There is a bronze dinosaur to photograph for free in the city park a block away.

In 1913 an association mapped out the National Old Trails Road through Arizona, following Girand's route with two exceptions. The new route followed the railroad west from Gallup, New Mexico, via Lupton to Holbrook. At Kingman, the Old Trails Highway headed west across the Black Mountains to Oatman, a very important town at the time. Girand's route between Springerville and Holbrook became a branch of the Old Trails Road. When the national highway system was laid out, the main National Old Trails main route, at the time unpaved, was chosen to carry Route 66.

On March 12, 1928, the 127 remaining runners in the Bunion Derby were ferried into Arizona and they crossed into New Mexico on March 23. The runners went from the Mojave Desert to the howling winds, snow, and ice of the mountains around Flagstaff, where they struggled even more due to the altitude.

The Dust Bowl refugees of the 1930s struggled across the mountains and deserts of Arizona too, often to be turned back at the California line if they didn't have money or a job. Arizona officials accused California of trying to "dump hoboes" back into the state. Some picked cotton in Arizona to earn enough money to make it to the Promised Land. In

Arizona, the road was a lifeline for those who made a living selling supplies, gas, and food, and some found work on the road itself. The last segment of Route 66 to be paved in Arizona was at Crozier Canyon, a 3.9-mile project completed on July 13, 1937.

During World War II, Route 66 was vital for moving troops and equipment to installations such as the Navajo Army Depot at Bellemont, just west of Flagstaff. Another great migration took place, as people sought defense jobs in California. Rationing of tires and gasoline curtailed recreational traveling. The glory years of Route 66 began when the war ended.

After World War II, the popularity of Route 66 was proving to be its downfall. The torturous route through Oatman was bypassed in 1952. The new route returned to Girand's pathway south from Kingman through Yucca and Topock. In 1956, one out of every six traffic deaths in Arizona occurred on "Bloody 66." In 1959, eleven people died in one month on a stretch of Route 66 near Peach Springs.

Interstate 40 was completed around Flagstaff in 1968, between Ash Fork and Kingman in 1975, around Winslow in 1978, and past Holbrook in 1981. A bittersweet ceremony on October 13, 1984, marked the opening of Interstate 40 around Williams, the last community on Route 66 to be bypassed. In 1985, Route 66 was officially decertified. But "The Mother Road" didn't die.

Angel Delgadillo, a barber in Seligman, gathered a group of business owners who formed the Route 66 Association of Arizona in February 1987. With Angel as an unofficial spokesman dubbed the "Guardian Angel of Route 66," the group sparked a revival that spread along the entire highway. In November 1987, the Arizona Legislature designated Route 66 between Seligman and Kingman as "Historic Route 66," a designation later applied to the entire route in Arizona. Today, travelers come from all over the world to experience a time when getting there was half the fun.

The wording on the giant kachina sign at the Pow Wow Trading Post in Holbrook was changed from "Motel" to "Rocks" when the motel units were converted to a rock shop. A medical marijuana dispensary later moved in to the remodeled building.

Above: Joe and Aggie Montano of Holbrook opened their café in 1943 and moved to this location in 1965. It has been in the family for three generations.

Above left: The rifle and powder horn on the Plainsman restaurant sign are a reminder of the 1880s, when the Hashknife Outfit cowboys of the Aztec Land and Cattle Company terrorized Holbrook. Twenty-six shooting deaths happened in 1886, when the population was about 250.

Left: Chester Lewis saw Frank Redford's Wigwam Village No. 2 at Cave City, Kentucky, and decided to build one of his own at Holbrook in 1950. The Wigwam closed in 1974 and was vacant until 1988 when the family restored the landmark.

Opposite: Many motels on Route 66 incorporated the highway into their names and signage. The 66 Motel in Holbrook sits atop the hill entering town and has been around since 1948.

The Jack Rabbit and Store for Men

Businesses along Route 66 resorted to all sorts of gimmicks to get travelers to stop, from cooked-up legends about Jesse James to fake prehistoric monsters. In Arizona, the competition was especially fierce. But two businesses teamed up to create simple images that would adorn billboards hundreds of miles away, one of which still brings in business decades later. One was a curvaceous cowgirl and the other a simple silhouette of a jackrabbit.

Wayne L. Troutner and James Taylor put Winslow and this part of Arizona on the map long before the Eagles song "Take It Easy" did. Troutner was a traveling salesman from State Center, Iowa. When his rounds brought him to Winslow, he decided to go into the cleaning business. He set his sights on a cleaning plant and clothing store operated by the Stevens Brothers and owned by William O'Hara of Boulder City, Nevada.

Troutner leased the cleaners from the Stevens Brothers in 1937 and bought the store from O'Hara in 1938. During World War II, he learned to fly, enlisted with the Seabees, and served in the Ship's Service Laundry. He changed the name of the business to Wayne L. Troutner's when he returned home after receiving a medical discharge in September 1944.

Wayne was an innovator from the beginning. He bought an airplane and soon was flying across northern Arizona to pick up laundry from other towns and the Indian reservations. The airborne laundry service only lasted a couple of years before a mishap at the airport in Show Low damaged his airplane beyond repair.

On July 14, 1950, Troutner opened his remodeled men's wear store and cleaners, handing out free orchids to the first five hundred ladies. He said he made the offer because mothers and wives purchased most of the clothes for men and boys. The cleaning plant moved to the back of the building and one section of the men's store focused on western clothing.

By that time, James Taylor had established his Jack Rabbit Trading Post sixteen miles (twenty-six kilometers) east of Winslow in a cinder block building at Joseph City. The Santa Fe Railroad built the structure. During the 1930s, it had housed the Arizona Herpetorium, but the snakes had been gone for years. Taylor put a billboard

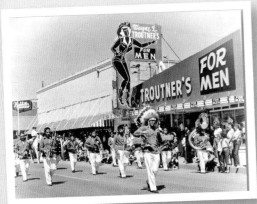

Old Trails Museum

up in front of the trading post featuring the black silhouette of a jackrabbit on a yellow background with large red letters shouting "Here It Is!"

Both businesses were doing well, but their owners had bigger things in mind. In November 1952, Troutner was planning another expansion when a man who was leasing an apartment from him in Winslow suggested he needed a new mascot. His tenant was James Taylor of the Jack Rabbit.

They enlisted the help of local sign painter Charles Holm and put together their ideas. Holm made the drawings used to apply for a trademark from the Arizona Secretary of State's Office on January 18, 1953. The new Troutner's Store for Men opened on February 6, 1953, and the new logo and big sign were ready.

The three men came up with another silhouette, this one of a buxom cowgirl clad in cut-off Levi's, a Western shirt, hat, and Acme boots sold at the store.

Taylor and Troutner decided to team up and plaster the highways with billboards featuring the black bunny and the cutie cowgirl. The Jack Rabbit boards listed the mileage to the post and nothing more. Only the cryptic caption "For Men, Winslow, Arizona" appeared under Troutner's cowgirl. It didn't take long to get a reaction. Some thought the billboards were for a strip club—or worse. Letters poured into the newspapers, and a Catholic Church official in Santa Fe even weighed in.

Both business owners posted the boards as far away as Springfield, Missouri. They had a way of turning up even thousands of miles away. A soldier apparently posted one in a barracks in Guam, and they were also seen as far away as Philadelphia, Chicago, and New York. Troutner chuckled all the way to the bank. It was reported that the billboards turned Troutner's Store for Men into a business bringing in a quarter million dollars each year.

Taylor even branched out with a line of perfume, "For Men" and "For Gals." There were "For Men" toiletries, including an aftershave and soap. Wayne and his wife Beth hit the road to promote the products while store manager Carnacion Chacon kept an eye on things with longtime employee Phillus Chavez. They later leased the store.

In 1984, the business was sold to Chacon's son Eddie. The name was changed to Eddie Chacon's Clothing Company and the sign was painted over. The store eventually went bankrupt and was destroyed by a fire blamed on an electrical problem on March 3, 1994.

The signs for the Jack Rabbit made the place irresistible, especially after travelers had been counting down the miles for hours. The trading post also became known for its sweet cherry cider. James Glenn Blansett took over the trading post in 1961. He had built the Pacific Motel and Union 76 station at Joseph City in 1947 and would go on to serve as an Arizona state senator from 1958 to 1968. Perhaps it's just a coincidence that the Jack Rabbit managed to end up with its own exit from Interstate 40.

Blansett passed the Jack Rabbit to his son and daughter in-law, Phil and Patricia Blansett. Cynthia and Antonio Jaquez, their daughter and son-in-law, now operate the trading post. At the Jack Rabbit, the original sign still stands across the highway, the cherry cider is served ice cold, and the bunny now adorns everything from T-shirts to underwear. The signs may be just simple silhouettes, but they have been bringing in business for more than six decades now.

Above: The 1972 Eagles hit "Take It Easy" made Winslow synonymous with the phrase "Standing on the Corner." Standing on the Corner Park includes a statue of a musician and a mural of a girl "in a flatbed Ford" slowing down to take a look. Winslow is also home to La Posada, the last of the great Fred Harvey hotels to be constructed.

Left: Meteor Junction was also once the bailiwick of the colorful "Rimmy Jim" Giddings and his trading post. Giddings erected signs saying he kept a graveyard for salesmen and placed an intercom beneath the outhouse seats to startle unsuspecting travelers.

Meteor Crater still attracts throngs of tourists. The Hopi believed a god who was cast from heaven caused this massive crater. White settlers discovered it in 1871, and at the time it was believed to have been of volcanic origin. Meteor Crater is 4,150 feet (1,266 meters) across, three miles (five kilometers) around the top, and 570 feet (174 meters) deep. The rim rises more than 150 feet (46 meters) above the surrounding desert.

Philadelphia mining engineer Daniel Moreau Barringer set up mining equipment at the crater in 1903. Barringer was ridiculed when he said a meteor created the crater. He spent the rest of his life and much of his private capital searching for the meteor, finding only fragments. Barringer's theory was accepted after he died in 1929.

Left: Six trading posts were located between Winslow and Winona: The Hopi House, Meteor City, Rimmy Jim's, Two Guns, Toonerville, and Twin Arrows. Twin Arrows was originally the Canyon Padre Trading Post and included a prefabricated 1951 Valentine diner. Two phone poles painted like arrows served as a sign to mark the entrance.

Right: Thousands of years ago, a massive meteorite fell to earth in present-day Arizona. By the Route 66 era, it was a major tourist attraction. Meteor City Trading Post owner Jack Newsum posted a sign on Route 66 reading "Population 1" and changed it to "Population 2" when he married. *Old Trails Museum*

Below: Taxidermist and sportsman Dean Eldridge opened a museum east of Flagstaff to hold his massive collection of mounts and curiosities in 1931. It became a nightclub in 1936, and Don and Thorna Scott made it a famous country music venue. Museum Club owner Don Scott killed himself after his wife Thorna died tragically, and their spirits are said to haunt the classic roadhouse to this day. In the background is the sign for Starlight Lanes, the Museum Club's neighbor since 1957.

Under the Sign of Two Guns

Route 66 crosses Canyon Diablo and the old route swings through the ruins of Two Guns, a historic and haunting spot that some think is cursed.

At first, Two Guns looks like the burned-out ruins of a 1960s or 1970s campground and gas station, blackened by fire and covered by graffiti. The words "Mountain Lions" are painted on the crumbling wall of an abandoned roadside zoo. But there's something else, an almost palpable feeling of dread, a feeling something terrible happened here. Two Guns has a long and bloody history.

The blood first flowed at the spot ten miles (sixteen kilometers) west of Winslow in 1878, when murderous Apaches raided Navajo settlements and escaped again and again. One day, a Navajo scout felt cool air coming from the ground and heard talking. He got down off his pony and realized he had tracked the raiders to their hiding spot, a cave tucked away in the canyon.

His fellow Navajo shot the guards and surrounded the only way out of the cave. They gathered brush and sticks and stuffed the cave entrance full. Then they set it on fire. From inside the cave came the sound of agonized horses and the death chants of the men. The Apache slaughtered their horses in hopes the blood would staunch the flames. All forty-two men in the cave died horribly.

The canyon was silent until construction of the Atlantic & Pacific, later Santa Fe Railroad, was halted at Canyon Diablo in 1881–1882 due to financial difficulties. A town sprang up that was larger than Flagstaff and said to be wilder than Tombstone. Hell Street in Canyon Diablo was lined with fourteen saloons, ten gambling dens, and four brothels. The first marshal was killed five hours after being sworn in. The longest-serving marshal lasted for thirty days before he was gunned down. Even the madams shot at each other. The town died as soon as the bridge was finished.

Another bizarre Two Guns tale began unfolding on the night of April 7, 1905. Two cowboys, John Shaw and Bill Smythe, walked into the Wigwam Saloon in Winslow, bellied up to the bar, and ordered a couple of drinks. They noticed a dice game going on and a few hundred dollars on the table. They pulled their guns, took the money, and ran toward the train yards, leaving a trail of silver dollars.

A posse caught up with them at Canyon Diablo on April 8. A shootout ensued and Smythe was wounded and captured. But Shaw was killed and buried on the spot in a donated pine box. A total of $271 in silver dollars was recovered.

The following evening some of the former Hashknife cowboys at the Wigwam were discussing the fact that Shaw should have had a chance to finish his drink. About fifteen of them headed for Canyon Diablo—

The entrance to the roadside zoo.

accompanied by a bottle of whiskey and a Kodak box camera—where they dug up Shaw. He actually appeared to be wearing a mischievous smile when they propped him up, gave him a last drink, and took his photo. The pictures were displayed on the walls of the Wigwam Saloon in Winslow until the building was torn down in the 1940s.

In 1924, Earl Cundiff opened his Canyon Lodge store and camp where the National Old Trails Road wound its way down to the bridge over Canyon Diablo. In March 1925, he leased it to the mystical Harry "Indian" Miller. Miller had lived among the Philippine headhunters and worked in silent films. Billing himself as "Chief Crazy Thunder," he built a roadside zoo, partnered with Hopi "Chief Joe" Sekakuku, and named the complex Fort Two Guns after a film starring his pal William S. Hart.

Miller strung some lights and built a wooden walkway to the cave. He cleaned the bones out, constructed some fake prehistoric ruins, and then placed the skulls of the dead Apache in strategic spots near the cave entrance to add to the effect.

The tourists snapped up soft drinks and snacks as they watched Chief Joe's Indian dances and met the animals in the zoo, including a bobcat, an eagle, a four-horned Navajo sheep, and a javelina.

On March 3, 1926, Miller shot and killed his landlord, Earl Marion Cundiff. Cundiff was unarmed, but Miller claimed self-defense and was acquitted. Harry Miller was never forgiven by some locals for shooting Earl Cundiff and was later convicted of defacing Cundiff's tombstone, which read "Killed by Indian Miller." Facing more legal troubles and claiming to be haunted by visions, Miller left in 1930 to open another business with fake Indian ruins at the Cave of the Seven Devils, on Route 66 near Gallup, New Mexico.

Earl Cundiff's widow married Phillip Hesch in 1934. Route 66 was relocated in 1938 and Hesch moved some of the buildings to the new highway to serve as store, station, and residence. He reestablished the zoo behind the store.

Benjamin Dreher took over in 1963 and constructed Two Gun Town, a campground, motel, restaurant, bar, and service station along the new Interstate 40. Access to the cave and ruins were restricted to registered guests at the campground. Guided tours and stagecoach rides were available.

Explosions in the early hours of August 1, 1971 shattered the tranquility. Two Guns was ablaze, and the gas tanks had exploded. Interstate 40 was shut down until the flames were brought under control. Dreher, perhaps the latest victim of the curse, walked away and abandoned Two Guns to the elements and the vandals.

Occasionally, a Route 66 traveler will venture onto the property despite the "no trespassing signs," the shattered glass, and the nails sticking out of the broken wood. They take their photos and quickly leave, making sure they don't become the latest chapter in the sad history of Two Guns.

The haunting ruins of the roadside zoo remain today.

Above: The Monte Vista Hotel has been a Flagstaff landmark since 1927. The Babbitt Brothers Building was constructed in 1888, and the building has been restored to its original appearance.

Right: Winona isn't actually a town, more of a trading post and service station. And the signs are nothing special. But the song "(Get Your Kicks on) Route 66" reminds us "don't forget Winona," so it gets a mention here. Winona earned a spot in the song because it nearly rhymes with Arizona.

OAK CREEK RAND CANYON 88 MI

LAKE MARY 8
CLARKDALE 53
JEROME 59
PRESCOTT 93

3 WILLIAMS
ASH FORK
PRESCOTT
KINGMAN

VIA
OAK CREEK
CANYON

ALTERNATE US 89   US 66

COTTONWOOD 50   WILLIAMS 33
CLARKDALE 53   ASHFORK 50
JEROME 58   KINGMAN 162
PRESCOTT 92   PRESCOTT 103

Above: The Western Hills Motel and Coffee Shop in Flagstaff opened in 1953, and the impressive sign was once animated to make it look like the wheels of the wagon were turning. The sign was originally painted blue.

While in Flagstaff, watch for Granny's Closet, formerly the Lumberjack Café. The café was the home of a pair of giant lumberjacks, the first of the roadside Muffler Men: huge fiberglass figures that once advertised all manner of businesses on the American roadside.

Left: Eddie Wong opened the Grand Canyon Café in 1938 and ran it with his brother Albert. The beautiful streamlined façade was added in 1950, and the Grand Canyon Café is still serving locals and Route 66 travelers today.

Opposite: This marker stood at the west end of Flagstaff, where US Highway 66 and US Highway 89 and 89A split. The US Highway 180 turnoff from Route 66 to the Grand Canyon lies a few miles to the east, while the Arizona Highway 64 turnoff to the national park is thirty miles (forty-six kilometers) west.

Above: A roadway from the National Old Trails Road (later Route 66) to the Grand Canyon opened in 1921, and Art Anderson and Don McMillan opened a store at the junction in Parks. It is now the Parks in the Pines General Store.

Williams was the last community on Route 66 to be bypassed. Bobby Troup was there to perform a bittersweet rendition of "(Get Your Kicks on) Route 66" when Interstate 40 opened on October 13, 1984.

Above right: The World Famous Sultana Bar in Williams opened in 1912 and has held a liquor license continually longer than any other watering hole in the state of Arizona. The Sultana Theater in the building started out showing silent films.

Right: The Turquoise Tepee in Williams is located in the historic building with a rock façade that once housed the Beacon Café. A tall tower supported the old café sign.

Far right: Between Williams and Ash Fork, Route 66 drops 1,200 feet (366 meters) in seven miles (eleven kilometers) before emerging onto the plain. Some of the abandoned alignments of Route 66 in this area are now bike trails.

Ash Fork was a busy place before the Santa Fe Railroad moved the mainline away in 1950. The opening of Interstate 40 in 1979 was another devastating blow. A fire on November 20, 1977, and another on October 7, 1987, virtually wiped out the business district. Today, the quiet town boasts of being the Flagstone Capital of the World.

Above: A 1960 DeSoto sits atop a former gas station in Ash Fork. *Carol Highsmith/ Library of Congress*

Above left: Interstate 40 opened on September 22, 1978, but the town of Seligman refused to die, mostly due to the "Angel of Route 66," Angel Delgadillo. The barber and businessman spearheaded the formation of the Historic Route 66 Association of Arizona in 1987, which started the Route 66 revival. Angel and his wife Vilma operate the Original Route 66 Gift Shop and visitor center.

Left: Angel's brother, Juan Delgadillo, opened the Snow Cap Drive-In in 1953. He was known for his showmanship and sense of humor, including a menu offering "Dead Chicken," fake door handles, and a mustard bottle that squirted yellow string.

Signs at the Snow Cap Drive-In read "Sorry— We're Open," and offer "Slightly Used Napkins and Straws." The lot is filled with vintage Route 66–era signage and old cars. Juan Delgadillo died on June 2, 2004, but his family carries on the tradition.

Top: The longest remaining unbroken stretch of Route 66 begins at Exit 139 on Interstate 40 between Ash Fork and Seligman and runs 162 miles (261 kilometers) to Topock. Seligman was originally known as Prescott Junction, founded in 1886 and later renamed for railroad financier Jesse Seligman.

Above: Seligman served as inspiration for the fictional town of Radiator Springs in the movie *Cars.* The community's preserved Route 66 heritage, funky shops, and sense of humor make it a popular tourist stop.

Right: The awesome sign at the Stagecoach 66 Motel in Seligman dates to the 1960s, when it was the Bil-Mar-Den Motel.

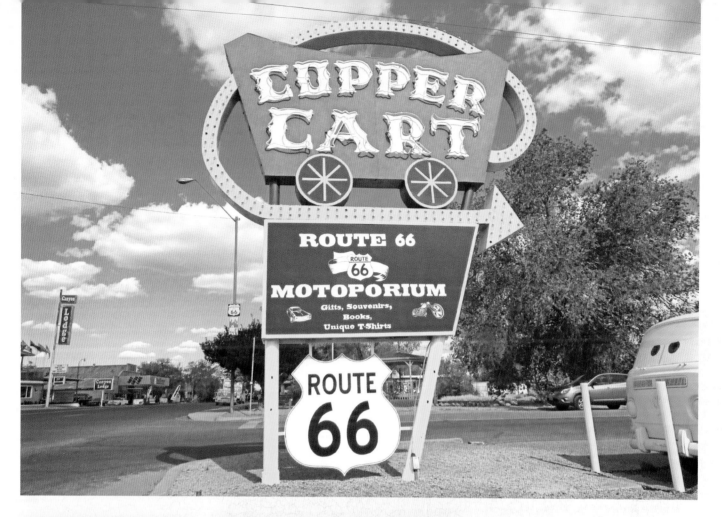

Above: The Copper Cart Restaurant in Seligman was in business from 1950 until 2013 and hosted the meeting that led to the organization of the Historic Route 66 Association of Arizona.

Left: Its sign looks great and the Historic Route 66 Motel in Seligman still gets good reviews. If you are hungry, it is right next door to the Road Kill Café.

Far left: The Supai Motel in Seligman opened in 1952 and takes its name from the nearby Havasupai Reservation. The vintage sign advertises "New Color TVs."

Top: In 1927, Walter Peck was on his way to a poker game when he stumbled and nearly fell into a deep cave entrance. Peck used a winch to lower tourists into the cave, known as Yampai Caverns and then Coconino Caverns. The name was changed to Dinosaur Caverns in 1957 and Grand Canyon Caverns in 1962.

Right: During his 1857 expedition, Lt. Edward Beale named a spring Truxton, which was his mother's maiden name. Truxton was little more than a railroad-watering stop until Clyde McCune opened a service station and Donald Dilts opened a café in October 1951. Many of the businesses were abandoned when Interstate 40 opened. These signs and weathered cars provide a photo opportunity. *Carol Highsmith/ Library of Congress*

Above: Mildred Barker ran The Frontier Motel and Café at Truxton from 1957 until shortly before her death in 2012. Allen Greer and Stacy Moores later took over and partly restored the Frontier.

Above left: John F. Miller built the first hotel in Las Vegas, Nevada. He opened El Trovatore at Kingman in 1939, the first air-conditioned motel in the state. New owner Sam Fisher resurrected the fading motel in 2011.

Above: Lieutenant Beale and his camels came through the Kingman area while surveying the wagon road in 1857, and a water source west of the town was named Beale Springs. A railroad siding was established here in 1882 and named for Lewis Kingman, the surveyor for the railroad.

A banner declaring Kingman the Gateway to Boulder Dam was once draped across Front Street. In 1955, the street was renamed in honor of Andy Devine, the raspy character actor from Kingman best known as Guy Madison's sidekick in the Wild Bill Hickok TV series.

Above right: The Kingman Club opened in 1944 but closed years ago, and the sign went dark. In 2015, Stacy Thomson renovated the building and opened the House of Hops, offering thirty-two different beers on tap. It cost $20,000 to restore the sign.

Left: The Hilltop Motel offers the "Best View in Kingman," overlooking the Hualapai Mountains.

Above : The Pony Soldier Motel opened in 1963, and its sign featuring a flashing and swooping neon arrow was modified when the name changed to the Route 66 Motel. It faded over the years but has been restored.

Left: Cool Springs was an oasis for travelers from 1926 until the new highway opened. The ruins were blown up for an action film before Ned Leuchtner rebuilt the landmark.

Route 66 climbs 1,400 feet (427 meters) in nine miles (fourteen kilometers) over Sitgreaves Pass. The west side of the grade plunges 700 feet (214 meters) in two miles (three kilometers) to the ruins of the old mining town of Goldroad. In the days of gravity-fed carburetors, locals would drive up the hill backward.

Top left: Prospector Lowell "Ed" Edgarton established Ed's Camp in 1919. The ruins remain where Original Route 66 begins its climb into the Black Mountains west of Kingman.

Top right: Local legend says Clark Gable and Carol Lombard spent their honeymoon at the Oatman Hotel in 1939. The ghost of a miner named Oatie is also said to haunt the hotel, which opened as the Hotel Durlin in 1902.

Above: Oatman is named for Olive Oatman, held captive for five years by American Indians (probably Western Yavapais and then Mohaves) after her family was massacred. The area population soared to twenty thousand before the mines closed. New Route 66 bypassing Oatman opened on September 17, 1952. Within twenty-four hours, six of the seven gas stations in town had closed. The population fell to about sixty.

Oatman now survives on tourism. The old prospectors turned their burros loose when they were no longer needed, and the descendants now roam and sometimes rule the streets. Colorful shops and cafés line the main street and shots ring out from staged gunfights.

Left: Route 66 originally crossed the Colorado River on the graceful National Old Trails Arch Bridge, which now carries a natural gas pipeline. Traffic was shifted to the former railroad bridge, shown here, in 1947. Interstate 40 replaced this bridge. Blue shields were used to mark westbound Route 66 in Arizona.

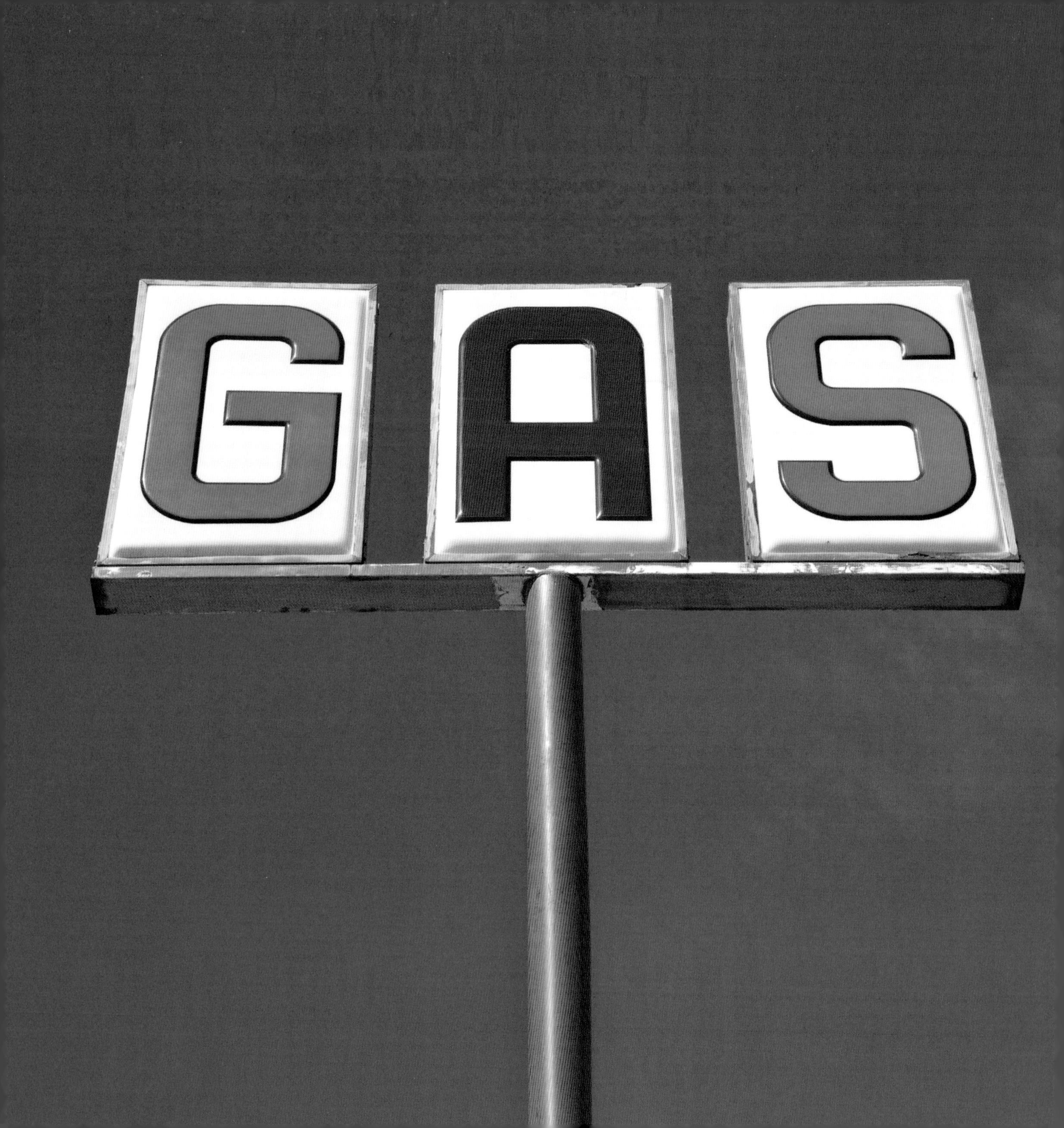
GAS

Chapter 8

The End of the Road

They've been coming since James Marshall first spotted a glint of gold at Sutter's Mill. Waves of people have headed west in search of opportunity, dreams of stardom, and golden sunshine in California. During much of the twentieth century, Route 66 was the road to those dreams.

Some of those dreamers might have been disappointed at their first glimpse. After a grueling journey through the Black Mountains and across the desert in Arizona, they could look west across the Colorado River toward the jagged peaks of the Needles to see what was to come. Ahead lay the vast and brutal Mojave Desert.

Few inhabitants were in the desolate land crossed by the Old Mojave Trail until the railroads came. The Atlantic & Pacific (Santa Fe) Railroad reached the Colorado in 1883, and a line was completed through the Cajon Pass to connect with the A and P at Waterman Junction in 1885. The town would be renamed in honor of the president of the Santa Fe, William Barstow Strong. The railroad established water stops strung out at regular intervals across the desert at Goffs, Fenner, Essex, Danby, Cadiz, Chambless, Amboy, Bagdad, Ludlow, and Newberry.

In 1895, California had become the second state in the nation to establish a state transportation agency, creating the Bureau of Highways to make recommendations to the state legislature on a state highway

Above: Fender's River Road Resort is on the Colorado River and is a great place to escape the desert heat. They bill themselves as "the funky 1960s-era resort," complete with the vintage sign.

Opposite: A promising gas sign in California's Mojave Desert. *trekandshoot/Shutterstock*

Top: Curving into Needles, Route 66 passes the Palms Motel and its neat little cottages dating from the 1920s. The covered wagon originally served as the sign for the El Rancho Needles Motel.

Above: The Route 66 Motel in Needles opened in 1946 but began to fade when Interstate 40 opened in 1970. It has operated as apartments for years. A private fundraising effort led by Ed Klein brought in money to restore the sign in 2012.

system. In 1915 the road from Barstow through Victorville and Cajon Pass into San Bernardino was incorporated into the state system designated as LRN 31. When Route 66 was commissioned in 1926, the highway was paved from Victorville all the way to Los Angeles. A gravel road from Daggett to Victorville opened that fall.

Travelers had already been using the Cajon Pass for centuries by the time Route 66 was commissioned. The road had been hard surfaced back in 1916. It has since been realigned, widened, or wiped out in several places. But a beautiful section of the old four-lane route through the Blue Cut and along Cajon Creek and the railroad waits at the Cleghorn Road exit off Interstate 15.

The 1930s were the decade of the great westward migration and a decade of change along the route. The Dust Bowl refugees were not welcomed with open arms. Many were turned back at the dreaded Agricultural Inspection Station on Route 66 at Daggett, which also doubled as a place to screen out the "undesirables." If the migrants made it to Barstow, they had to decide whether to head north toward the agricultural jobs in the Joaquin Valley or south toward the Imperial Valley. But whichever way they went, they faced low wages, poor living conditions, and derision as "Okies." It's estimated that more than one-third just decided to continue west to Los Angeles where they also faced hostility. For two months in 1936, the LAPD went so far as to set up a "bum blockade" at sixteen locations along the Arizona, Nevada, and Oregon borders.

At this time, engineers were working to make Route 66 a modern and safe highway, abandoning the section of the National Old Trails Road that ran from Needles northwest to Goffs and then down to Essex. The loop through Goffs was bypassed in 1931, and another new route would connect Essex with Amboy.

The US 66 Highway Association had been kept busy after the Bunion Derby transcontinental footrace, printing up brochures and press releases touting 66 as *the* way west to the paradise of California. The association placed its first advertisement in the July 16, 1932, issue of the *Saturday Evening Post.* The ad urged travelers to take 66 to the Olympic Games in Los Angeles. They found the route through the San Gabriel Valley towns was also changing. Foothill Boulevard between

San Bernardino and Pasadena had been widened to a four-lane modern highway by 1937.

Original Route 66 left Pasadena on Fair Oaks Drive and turned onto Huntington Drive, the historic old Adobe Road. The route continued onto Mission and then Broadway to terminate at Seventh and Broadway in Los Angeles. There were transitional alignments that took different paths, including one that used the historic Colorado Street Bridge and Eagle Rock Boulevard.

A major change came on January 1, 1936, when the western terminus of the route was extended from downtown Los Angeles west via Sunset Boulevard to Santa Monica Boulevard, turning on to Lincoln Boulevard (US Highway 101 Alternate) and officially ending at Olympic. Although it makes a nice sentimental end to the journey, a bureaucrat would point out that a US highway had to terminate at another highway, so 66 never extended officially to the Santa Monica Pier. But sentimentality sort of won in November 2009, when the Santa Monica Convention and Visitor's Bureau joined other groups in erecting a sign declaring Santa Monica Pier to be the "End of the Trail."

A second wave of westward migration swept along Route 66 during World War II, as families headed west in search of jobs at plants such as Kaiser Steel in Fontana and Douglas Aircraft in Santa Monica. The Rose Bowl in Pasadena was used as an assembly point for ethnic Japanese being shipped to relocation camps.

The Mojave was turned into the US Army Desert Training Center to train soldiers for desert fighting against the Germans in North Africa. More than five hundred thousand soldiers trained at one of the thirteen divisional camps spread across eighteen thousand square miles (46,600 kilometers square). The tank tracks are still visible in the desert.

After the war, GIs returned with their families to vacation at Disneyland or the beaches. During the 1950s, Route 66 was bypassed at a fast clip. In 1958, work began on the Foothill Freeway (Interstate 210) paralleling old 66 along Foothill Boulevard through the San Gabriel Valley and Pasadena. Interstate 40 replaced the old route through the Mojave. The last freeway segment replacing 66 was completed in 1974, when Interstate 15 was linked with Interstate 10 at Ontario.

Top: The vertical sign at Cub's Liquor stands out against the nighttime desert sky on Broadway in Needles.

Above: Goffs, population twenty-three, offers a restored 1914 schoolhouse with displays of mining relics, old cars, and signs. This section was originally the National Old Trails Road and original Route 66, bypassed in 1931.

Top: Past Chambless, the Road Runner's Retreat opened toward the end of the Route 66 era and was killed by Interstate 40 in the 1970s. This oasis was spruced up for a 1980s car commercial and then left to the elements again.

Above: In Ludlow, the businesses moved a block north when the interstate was constructed in 1972, leaving the ruins of this old mining town and the original Ludlow Café to fade into the desert.

Right: At Amboy, Roy's has been awaiting travelers wearied by a journey across the Mojave since 1927, and the sign featured in commercials and movies went up in 1956. The owner of the Juan Pollo chain, Albert Okura, bought the entire "town" in 2005.

Above left: Daggett was a very busy place during the borax mining days. The Desert Market, the only store for miles, was rebuilt with concrete after the original building burned in 1908.

Top: When the Santa Fe Railroad expanded in 1925, the entire business district of Barstow moved to the new Main Street. The Barstow Motor Court from that era grew into the Route 66 Motel.

Above: Tourists come from around the world to see the setting for the 1987 film *Bagdad Café* at Newberry Springs. It was originally the Sidewinder Café. The actual vanished town of Bagdad was fifty miles (eight-one kilometers) to the east.

Left: The Palm Café in Barstow opened in 1960 in a converted gas station and closed in 2013. It was remodeled into a doctor's office in 2015, and the neon sign was taken down.

Above: West of Helendale, Elmer Long has assembled vintage signs, bottles, and all sorts of artifacts into a folk art display in the middle of the desert known as the "Bottle Tree Ranch."

Right: Polly Gas stations could be found in Southern California from 1935 until they were taken over by Gulf in 1960. This sign still stands west of Helendale.

Below: A neon arch marks the entrance to historic Old Town in Victorville, where the California Route 66 Museum is located. The arch features the city seal.

Left: Emma Jean's Holland Burger Café has been serving Route 66 travelers in Victorville since 1947 and is still in the family today. It was featured in the movie *Kill Bill: Volume 2*.

Below: In 1940, brothers Richard and Maurice McDonald opened a barbeque restaurant on E Street in San Bernardino that developed into the first McDonald's. It was torn down in 1971, but Albert Okura has turned the site into a museum celebrating the history of the fast-food giant.

Bottom left: San Bernardino's Dream Inn was once the Sharene Motel. The original sign was painted over and the neon removed in 2013, when new owners took over the property and changed the name to the Dream Inn.

Above: As Foothill approaches the Rialto city limits, look to the right for a Route 66 treasure, the restored Wigwam Motel. The Wigwam in San Bernardino was the last one of seven to be constructed and was opened in 1949. It later fell into decline, advertising "Do it in a Tee Pee," but has been resurrected and maintained immaculately by Kumar Patel and his family.

Right: Rancho Cucamonga is proud of its Route 66 heritage, and the 1915 Cucamonga Service Station has been restored. William "Billy" Rubottom's Mountain View Inn at Rancho Cucamonga opened in 1848. The current structure, now the Sycamore Inn, was completed in 1920. Chuck and Linda Keagle took over in 2002 and carry on the tradition.

Left: The Magic Lamp Inn at Rancho Cucamonga was originally Lucy and John's Café. In 1955, the remodeled restaurant opened as the Sycamore Inn. Employees came up with their ideas for a name and the winner was chosen in a drawing.

Top: A nicely maintained historic Route 66 property that opened in 1957, the Palm Tropics in Glendora is still in its original cottage-style configuration and has kept its classic sign.

Above: Early 66 through Glendora followed Amelia, Foothill, and Citrus. The later alignment curves onto Alosta Avenue, now labeled as Route 66. The Golden Spur Restaurant in Glendora started out as a ride-up hamburger stand for customers on horseback in 1918. The steakhouse opened in 1954. The exterior has been altered, but the 1954 sign is still there.

Above left: La Paloma Restaurant has been operating in La Verne since 1966. The building dates to 1928 and was originally Wilson's Sandwich Shop.

Left: Both alignments merge as Foothill Boulevard into Azusa, where the marquee of the old Foothill Drive-In remains even though the theatre is gone. The drive-in opened in December 1961 and closed in 2001 when the site was purchased by Azusa Pacific University for use as a parking lot.

Right: Foothill becomes Huntington Drive into Duarte. The original route went north on Shamrock, west on Foothill through Monrovia. The Aztec Hotel, opened in 1924, is located on this alignment. Designer Robert Stacy Judd mixed Mayan Revival, art-deco, and Spanish Colonial styles. Stacy called it the Aztec because he thought the public was less familiar with the Mayan culture. The hotel closed for renovations in 2012.

Below: The Pasadia Motor Hotel was once billed as "Pasadena's Newest and Finest." The motel has faded substantially, and the repainted sign now reads "The Pasada Motel."

Above: The route over Huntington turns onto Colorado Boulevard and continues past the Santa Anita Park and Racetrack into Pasadena. Since 1959, the Saga Motor Hotel has been a landmark on East Colorado Boulevard right on the Rose Parade Route. Designed by Harold Zook, the Saga has held up well and been featured in the TV shows *CSI* and *Dexter.*

Above left: Pasadena is known as the home of the Rose Bowl and the annual Rose Parade. The Rose Bowl Motel is actually in Los Angeles.

Left: The Route 66 traveler has a choice of several alignments leaving Pasadena starting with the Alternate 66 Route over the amazing Colorado Street Bridge and then down Figueroa. The early alignment follows Fair Oaks Avenue, Huntington, and Mission to Broadway. Fair Oaks Pharmacy and Soda Fountain opened in 1915 as the South Pasadena Pharmacy and was later known as the Raymond Pharmacy.

Since 1895, planners had envisioned a scenic parkway connecting Pasadena with Los Angeles along the west edge of the Arroyo Seco. Work began in 1938 on the Arroyo Seco Parkway. The first limited-access high-speed toll-free state highway in the United States opened on December 30, 1940, and one official said it would "solve traffic congestion for all time to come." It was extended to the Hollywood Freeway at the landmark four-level interchange in 1953 and carried Route 66 until 1964. The former route along Figueroa was designated as US Highway 66 Alternate.

Top: The iconic Hollywood sign is visible from Santa Monica Boulevard. *Los Angeles Times* publisher Harry Chandler built it to promote his Hollywoodland development in 1923. It was nearly demolished in 1944 before the city took it over and took down the last four letters.

Above: Irv's Burgers has been a tradition on Santa Monica Boulevard since 1950. The original stand, shown here, appeared on the cover of a Linda Ronstadt album. Irv's moved a few blocks to the east in 2014 when the original site was targeted for redevelopment.

Above center: The Paradise Motel, "In the center of L.A. and everything," still has some nice neon. It opened on Sunset Boulevard in 1946. The Paradise boasted a prime location where Highways 6 and 66 crossed the 101 and was once featured in the television show *The O.C.*

Above right: The Rialto Theater opened in 1917 and closed in 1987. But it reopened as an Urban Outfitters store in 2013, and the marquee was restored.

Right: Route 66 originally ended at Seventh and Broadway in the heart of the Los Angeles Theater District. The Loew's State Theatre opened in 1921 and has been repurposed as a church.

The public always felt that Route 66 ended at the Santa Monica Pier. It just took eighty-three years for someone to make it official. On November 11, 2009, the Route 66 Alliance, a group of 66 enthusiasts and business owners, declared the pier to be the western end of the route that began in Chicago. The group unveiled a replica of a sign that stood nearby in the 1930s, declaring "The End of the Trail." It's a place to reflect on the journey and those who came before.

When it was commissioned in 1926, Route 66 officially ended at Seventh and Broadway in downtown Los Angeles. In 1935, a movie studio erected a sign reading "End of the Trail" on the bluffs overlooking the Santa Monica Pier. That sign remained for years, bolstering the perception among the public that Route 66 ended at that point.

In 1936 the route was officially extended through Santa Monica, but not all the way to the ocean. Federal highway officials stuck to their rule that one US highway must end at the intersection with another. The official terminus became the intersection of Lincoln and Olympic Boulevards. (US 101A) Olympic and Lincoln was and still is a busy, exhaust-choked intersection. It's certainly no place for a photo op or sentimental reflection.

In 1952, Route 66 was dedicated as the Will Rogers Highway partly as a stunt to promote the movie *The Story of Will Rogers*. Signs marking the designation were placed at each state line along the way and the final one was placed beneath the palm trees in Palisades Park across from the intersection of Santa Monica Boulevard and Ocean Avenue and not far from where the movie sign had stood. That further cemented the idea that 66 ended at the ocean. From there, it was just two blocks to the pier.

Top: In the 1960s, the freeways were replacing Route 66, and the official western terminus moved even further from the ocean, to Colorado Boulevard at the Arroyo Seco Parkway in Pasadena. After Interstate 15 and Interstate 40 had been completed in 1975, it was moved all the way back to the California-Arizona border. In 1985, Route 66 officially ceased to exist. The movie sign had disappeared years before. But unofficially, Route 66 never died as travelers inspired by nostalgia or the mythical version of the road continued to seek it out.

Above: At the very end of the Santa Monica Pier, a display at Mannie Mendelson's shop memorializes his friend Bob Waldmire, the artist and free spirit who inspired many to travel Route 66. Bob passed away on December 16, 2009. This is a place to reflect on one's journey on Route 66, and our journey through life. Route 66 travelers often stand here for a moment as the sun sinks beneath the waves. They sigh and turn toward home.

Right: In 2009, a physical sign that 66 ended at the pier emerged when Dan Rice opened 66-to-Cali and was searching for a symbol for a T-shirt. He found the image of the old movie sign and knew it was perfect, so he brought the Route 66 Alliance and the City of Santa Monica together. Today, the sign is a magnet for tourists.

About Joe Sonderman

Joe Sonderman has authored eleven books on Route 66. He is the editor of the Route 66 Association of Missouri's *Show Me Route 66* magazine and is the author of many articles for *Route 66* magazine. He has also written books on the 1904 St. Louis World's Fair and two others on the history of St. Louis.

Additionally, Sonderman assisted the Autry Museum with its recent exhibition on Route 66 and is currently working with the Missouri History Museum on a Route 66 exhibit. He has a collection of more than ten thousand vintage Route 66 images, as well as hundreds of original photos.

About Jim Hinckley

Since his childhood, **Jim Hinckley** dreamed of being an author. After numerous detours into truck driving, mining, ranching, and a variety of other endeavors, he turned to writing a weekly column on automotive history for his local newspaper, the *Kingman Daily Miner*, in his adopted hometown of Kingman, Arizona.

From that initial endeavor more than twenty years ago, Hinckley has written extensively on his two primary passions: automotive history and travel. He is a regular contributor to *Route 66, American Road, Hemmings Classic Car,* and *Old Cars Weekly,* and he was an associate editor at *Cars & Parts*. Book reviews and original features on automotive history and travel can be found on his blog, www.route66chronicles.blogspot.com and on his popular podcast, Jim Hinckley's America & Route 66 Adventures.

Index